WRITERS AN

ISOBEL ⸱

Gener

WOMEN'S GOTHIC
FROM CLARA REEVE TO MARY SHELLEY

An illustration from a French edition of Clara Reeve's
The Old English Baron (Paris, 1800).

WOMEN'S GOTHIC

FROM CLARA REEVE TO MARY SHELLEY

E. J. Clery

Second Edition

Northcote House
in association with the
British Council

My thanks to John Birtwhistle, Nora Crook, Robert Miles, and Julie Shaffer for their comments on individual chapters. I am especially grateful to Susan Caroline Salaman for responding to the work-in-progress and making it a pleasure to write.

First published in 2000 by Northcote House Publishers Ltd, Horndon, Tavistock, Devon, PL19 9NQ, United Kingdom.
Tel: +44 (01822) 810066 Fax: +44 (01822) 810034.

Second edition 2004

British Library Cataloguing-in-Publication Data
A catalogue record for this book is available from the British Library

ISBN 0-7463-1144-3
Typeset by PDQ Typesetting, Newcastle-under-Lyme
Printed and bound in the United Kingdom by Athenaeum Press Ltd., Gateshead

Contents

Illustrations

Abbreviations

CAD   Ann Radcliffe, *The Castles of Athlin and Dunbayne*, ed. Alison Milbank (Oxford and New York: Oxford University Press, 1995).

DM   Joanna Baillie, *De Monfort: A Tragedy*, in *Seven Gothic Dramas 1789–1825*, ed. Jeffrey N. Cox (Athens, OH: Ohio University Press, 1992).

F.   Mary Shelley, *Frankenstein or The Modern Prometheus* (the 1818 text), ed. Marilyn Butler (Oxford and New York: Oxford University Press, 1994).

HS   Charlotte Dacre, *Hours of Solitude: A Collection of Original Poems, now first published*, intr. Donald Reiman (1805; repr. New York, 1978).

I.   Ann Radcliffe, *The Italian; or the Confessional of the Black Penitents, A Romance*, ed. Frederick Garber, intro. and notes E. J. Clery (Oxford and New York: Oxford University Press, 1998).

M.   Mary Shelley, *Matilda*, ed. Pamela Clemit, vol. 2 of *The Novels and Selected Works of Mary Shelley*, general ed. Nora Crook (London: William Pickering, 1996).

MU   Ann Radcliffe, *The Mysteries of Udolpho, A Romance*, ed. Bonamy Dobrée, intr. and notes Terry Castle (Oxford and New York: Oxford University Press, 1998).

O.   Joanna Baillie, *Orra* (1851; repr. Cambridge Chadwyck-Healey English Verse Drama Full-Text Database, 1994).

OEB   Clara Reeve, *The Old English Baron: A Gothic Story*, ed. James Trainer (London: Oxford University Press, 1967).

R.   Sophia Lee, *The Recess; or, A Tale of Other Times*, 3 vols. (1783–85; repr. New York: Arno Press, 1972).

RF   Ann Radcliffe, *The Romance of the Forest*, ed. Chloe Chard (Oxford and New York: Oxford University Press, 1986).

SR   Ann Radcliffe, *A Silician Romance*, ed. Alison Milbank
      (Oxford and New York: Oxford University Press, 1993).
V.   Mary Shelley, *Valperga: or, The Life and Adventures of
      Castruccio, Prince of Lucca*, ed. Tilottama Rajan (Peter-
      borough, Ontario: Broadview Press, 1998).
Z.   Charlotte Dacre, *Zofloya; or The Moor*, ed. Kim Ian Michasiw
      (Oxford and New York: Oxford University Press, 1997).

Introduction

A woman's story at a winter's fire,
Authorized by her grandam...

(Macbeth, III. iv. 65–6)

LADY MACBETH IN THE EIGHTEENTH CENTURY

The common picture we have of women writers in the Romantic period is one of concealment, restraint, fear of criticism, self-censorship. While the male poets issued their manifestos, dabbled in metaphysics, or cut a dash in fashionable drawing rooms, women were, if not invisible, then confined by circumstances, and by the more intangible prison of female propriety. There is Frances Burney, forced to burn her childhood scribblings on the orders of her father and, later in life, to accept an existence of mindless tedium as lady-in-waiting to the queen. Or Charlotte Smith, who escaped from a wretched marriage at the price of churning out sentimental novels 'like a galley slave tied to the oars', in order to support her nine children. Or most famously Jane Austen writing in the drawing room, hurriedly hiding away her manuscripts whenever a visitor entered, and publishing anonymously through her brother. It has been influentially argued that these unfavourable conditions left an indelible mark on their imaginations, and their style of writing, that it discouraged them from overt treatment of politics or philosophy in favour of a more safely 'feminine' focus on the domestic and the quotidien. The argument goes that women writers chose to specialize in the depiction of personal relations in realistic settings, rather than attempting to represent more exotic locales or great public events like their male contemporaries, and that they employed a language of refined moral sentiment and feeling rather than attempting abstract ideas or grand flights of imagination. Their forte was miniaturism, attention to detail.

In the first wave of feminist literary history, the rescue of women writers from obscurity tended to involve the construction of an alternative, repressed female tradition. The subordination of women in society was proposed not only as a way of explaining the neglect of women writers, but was also found to be the constant theme of their literary work. Like all attempts to redress the balance, the dualism of male and female traditions involves a simplification of the reality and fails to account for many aspects of women's writing in the period. It has notably distorted our understanding of women's achievements in Gothic writing. The current fascination with the Gothic genre in the academy and in the culture generally, has led to many studies of early female writers of Gothic, and almost invariably their works have been read as parables of patriarchy involving the heroine's danger from wicked father figures, and her search for the absent mother. Family relations yet again, though in a heightened form. In this way 'Female Gothic' can be absorbed into the notion of a distinctive women's tradition.

But what happens if we lay aside our assumptions about women's writing and look again at women's Gothic? What we find there suggests the need for another story: wild passions, the sublime, supernatural phenomena, violent conflict, murder and torture, sexual excess and perversion, outlandish settings, strange minglings of history and fantasy. We also need to look again at the response to these works. Were the writers vilified for their daring? No, in many cases they were praised. The six authors dealt with here – Clara Reeve, Sophia Lee, Ann Radcliffe, Joanna Baillie, Charlotte Dacre and Mary Shelley – all achieved either respectable critical success, or in the cases of Radcliffe and Baillie, fame and adulation. All of them signed their works with their own names at some stage in their careers, and in any case their authorship soon became common knowledge. All of them were successful professional writers, ambitious and innovative, openly courting the public with sensational material. And they were not alone. There were more than fifty women writers from the 1790s to the 1820s writing in what we now call the Gothic genre, which they knew more loosely and indiscriminately as, among other things, 'modern romance',[1] encompassing poetry, drama and fiction.

Gothic literature sees women writers at their most pushy and argumentative. Clara Reeve takes Walpole to task on the proper management of the supernatural in the preface to *The Old English Baron*. Harriet Lee, sister of Sophia, publicly denounces the management of Drury Lane for turning down her play *The Mysterious Marriage*, and claims precedence over 'Monk' Lewis for the idea of introducing a 'real ghost' on stage. The teenaged Charlotte Dacre shamelessly demands the patronage of Lewis, in the dedication of her first novel, *The Confessions of the Nun of St Omer*, which rivalled his work for lurid sensationalism. One of the things I hope to do in this book is to capture the sense of excitement, audacity and opportunism which accompanied the opening up of a new field of literary endeavour. Feminism has shown the flawed and partial nature of histories which neglect the lives and achievements of women. The project of recovery is now well advanced, but the task remains to rewrite mainstream history in order to show the real importance of women in every aspect of the political, economic, and cultural life of a society.

As a preliminary, the question needs to be asked, what empowered these authors, given that there were indeed considerable obstacles to the success of women in the literary sphere? In addition to stereotypes of the ridiculous and unfeminine bluestocking, they had to contend with the practical difficulties of inadequate education and family opposition, as well as their inexperience and inhibitions in the world of business. What gave women the confidence to experiment, attempt large effects, fly in the face of critical opinion, openly rival and emulate the achievements of their male peers? Ann Radcliffe has typically been painted as the most modest, even demure, of novelists. Yet her one existing piece of critical writing provides an excellent introduction to the vaulting ambitions of the female writers of Gothic, and the way in which their dreams were validated.

Radcliffe's essay 'On the Use of the Supernatural in Poetry' was first published in the *New Monthly Magazine* in 1826, three years after her death. It originally formed the prologue to her last novel, *Gaston de Blondeville* (written in 1802 and published in 1826). In it, she stages a dialogue on aesthetics between Mr

Simpson, a vulgar philistine, and Mr Willoughton, a man of sensibility who is obviously her mouthpiece. Mr Willoughton speaks the exalted language of Romantic poetic theory. He asks, Where is the successor to Shakespeare?: 'Where is now the undying spirit... that could inspire itself with various characters of this world, and create worlds of its own; to which the grand and the beautiful, the gloomy and the sublime of visible Nature, up-called not only corresponding feelings, but passions; which seemed to perceive a soul in every thing'.[2] The poet is accorded the power of a demiurge, a god-like creator, capable of uniting humanity and nature in an inspired harmony. The language used by Radcliffe is not uncommon in contemporary offerings to the cult of Shakespeare, but it is also strongly reminiscent of a passage from a poem published just a few years before, 'Lines composed a few miles above Tintern Abbey' (1798), where Wordsworth describes the 'sublime' gift of inspiration, 'that serene and blessed mood' in which

> we are laid asleep
> In body, and become a living soul:
> While with an eye made quiet by the power
> Of harmony, and the deeper power of joy,
> We see into the life of things.

(ll. 45–9)

The concern here, as in Radcliffe, is nothing less than the fate of poetry and genius in a modern world which militates against them.

It is telling that Radcliffe chooses to make this creative agency gender-neutral. And indeed, as the discussion progresses, the only living exponent of the 'undying spirit' of transformative poetry who is mentioned, turns out to be female: the great tragic actress Sarah Siddons. Pat Rogers has suggested that Siddons, by attracting praise in terms of the sublime 'extended the range of the feminine, that is, she made permissible the attribution to women of a less restricted and timid set of human qualities' and 'must have affected the way in which women were able to conduct themselves in ordinary life'.[3] Her 'male dignity' in performance made it possible to conceive of women as heroes and as historical agents. I will be arguing that, in precise ways, her example constitutes a Siddonian paradigm, an enabling condition for women's Gothic. Radcliffe's admiring

4

account of Siddons is an important instance of her adoption as a figurehead by women writers, and especially, as we will see, by women writing in the Gothic mode. The topic of Siddons's artistic genius, as it is raised by Radcliffe, becomes the opportunity for an assertion of women's capacity for sublimity in general. And beyond Siddons lies the unassailable 'cultural capital' of the national genius, Shakespeare.

Mention of Siddons arises in the context of a debate about the appropriate staging of the witches in *Macbeth*. Willoughton protests against the deflating effect of Scotch dress.

> So vexatious is the effect of the stage-witches upon my mind, that I should probably have left the theatre when they appeared, had not the fascination of Mrs Siddons's influence so spread itself over the whole play, as to overcome my disgust, and to make me forget even Shakspeare himself; while all consciousness of fiction was lost, and his thoughts lived and breathed before me in the very form of truth. Mrs Siddons, like Shakspeare, always disappears in the character she represents, and throws an illusion over the whole scene around her, that conceals many defects in the arrangements of the theatre.[4]

The view that Siddons was the living representative of tragedy, the incarnation of dramatic poetry, could be called a commonplace of the time. It was made official by Joshua Reynolds's famous portrait of her in the guise of the 'Tragic Muse'. In the figure of Siddons, the distinction between actor and poet was blurred. Siddons, Mr Willoughton remarks, is 'like Shakspeare'. A contemporary biographer of Siddons stated, 'Where there was little or no poetry, she made it for herself; and might be said to have become at once both the dramatist and the actress'.[5] But it is further and more daringly claimed in Radcliffe's dialogue that 'she would be the finest Hamlet that ever appeared',[6] superior even to her brother John Philip Kemble or indeed any male actor: 'she would more fully preserve the tender and refined melancholy, the deep sensibility, which are the peculiar charm of Hamlet, and which appear not only in the ardour, but in the occasional irresolution and weakness of his character – the secret spring that reconciles all his inconsistencies'.[7]

This gendered language suggests that the female artist is better equipped than the male to combine the two elements highlighted in Aristotle's definition of tragedy: pity and terror. There is a vital point at stake here. Radcliffe appears to accept the established model of tragic drama which includes its contrasting features of 'masculine' sublimity and 'feminine' sensibility, or the 'grand and the beautiful', as she puts it. Shakespeare, a male poet, has the ability to transcend and subsume this gender opposition; he can 'inspire himself with various characters of this world, and create worlds of his own'. The remarks on Siddons imply Radcliffe's belief that women were in general better able than men to perform the act of creative androgyny, to combine 'masculine' and 'feminine' feelings or effects in a unified whole. Later in the discussion Radcliffe makes a comparison of literary effects of horror, with the more subtle and suggestive effects of terror that resemble her favoured narrative methods. This has been taken as a veiled criticism of the work of her rival, 'Monk' Lewis. More immediately, Radcliffe underlines the application to her novels by using landscape description as a metaphor, in obvious reference to her own celebrated talents in that sphere.

> The strong light which shows the mountains of a landscape in all their greatness, and with all their rugged sharpness, gives them nothing of the interest with which a more gloomy tint would invest their grandeur; dignifying, though it softens, and magnifying, while it obscures.[8]

The image of the mountain is peculiarly resonant in Romantic-era culture. Mountains were the ultimate emblem of the natural sublime, and have often been taken, by analogy, to encode a masculinist prejudice. Radcliffe's point is that just as Siddons could take on the part of Hamlet, the high point of Shakespeare's genius, and surpass the achievements of male counterparts by inflecting it with sensibility, so she herself, as a writer of romance, could appropriate the grandest effects of literary art, and enhance them by softening and mystifying. What results (according to Radcliffe) is not a 'feminine' aesthetic but rather a truly universal aesthetic, enabled by women's greater powers of sympathetic androgyny.

'Romantic androgyny' is a term which has been introduced into critical discourse to describe the 'colonisation of the feminine' by male poets intent on defining a new aesthetic, which broke with the formal and thematic conventions of the past.[9] What a study of women's Gothic reveals is that incursions were not one-way, and that women writers of Gothic were likewise engaged in polemical revision of literary practice, involving the transgression of gender expectations. Siddons represented for them a female genius without bounds. For Sophia Lee and Joanna Baillie her influence extended to direct patronage, when she actively fought for performance of their plays at Drury Lane Theatre and acted in them herself. Others like Radcliffe admired from a distance, and simply made the connection with their own ambitions. Judith Pascoe in *Romantic Theatricality* has shown the way Siddons was taken as a role model for a whole generation of women writers; 'Siddons provides the most obvious model of female creative power'.[10] Her eminently respectable success – artistic and professional – gave great encouragement to all women seeking a public voice. In the next section, I will explore her special relevance for the Gothic, and women's Gothic in particular, through her interpretation of Lady Macbeth, her most famous role.

'THE EXCITEMENTS OF HELL'

It is only recently that the exemplary importance of Sarah Siddons in Romantic-era culture has begun to be recognized,[11] but the actress's contemporaries were in no doubt about her significance. When Coleridge came to write a series of 'Sonnets of Eminent Characters' for the newspaper the *Morning Chronicle* in 1794–5, his subjects were all male with the exception of Mrs Siddons, and mainly political. At the time he was ardently interested in the Treason Trials of the radicals Hardy, Tooke, Thelwall and Holcroft which were then taking place in London. The first sonnet of the series was addressed to the lawyer Erskine, who conducted a brilliant and successful defence involving the argument that the crime 'of imagining the death of the king' must equally have been committed by the prosecutors.[12] It is very probably an association of ideas that led Coleridge to celebrate the art of Siddons, most famous as the regicide Lady Macbeth. His praise of her suggests her inspirational role in the development of Gothic sensibility in the 1790s, and also the very topical nature of contagious emotion as a subject of discussion in the era of the French Revolution.[13]

7

Mrs Siddons

As when a child on some long Winter's night
Affrighted clinging to its Grandam's knees
With eager wond'ring and perturb'd delight
Listens strange tales of fearful dark decrees

Mutter'd to wretch by necromantic spell;
Or of those hags, who at the witching time
Of murky Midnight ride the air sublime,
And mingle foul embrace with fiends of Hell:

Cold Horror drinks its blood! Anon the tear
More gentle starts, to hear the Beldame tell
Of pretty Babes, that lov'd each other dear,
Murder'd by cruel Uncle's mandate fell:

Even such the shiv'ring joys thy tones impart,
Even so thou, SIDDONS! meltest my sad heart!

It is interesting first of all to note Coleridge's attention to Siddons's ability to combine the terrible and the tender, already noted in the passage from Radcliffe. Again, as in Radcliffe's account, Siddons's acting is presented as a form of creativity, above all through the power to excite strong emotions in the audience. However, Coleridge does not compare her with Shakespeare (or not explicitly: there are verbal allusions which will be discussed in a moment) but, more obscurely, with the art of the story-teller, and the oral tradition of ghost stories typically associated with 'old wives'. Why this analogy of the celebrated actress with the homely 'Grandam'? The connection requires some explanation for modern readers.

By the 1790s, ghost stories had undergone a revolution. Where once they had been banished from polite culture as a despised remnant of obsolete popular superstition, now they dominated the literary scene, a craze on a scale never known before. Coleridge's poem is a tribute to the extraordinary transvaluation of the supernatural, from low superstition to aesthetic resource. Earlier in the century the common view would have been that a taste for tales of the supernatural was the sign of a weak mind (hence the reference to women and children), now the supernatural was converted into an opportunity for asserting poetic vision beyond the mundane for the writer, and achieving a sublime experience of terror for

8

the audience. The process of conversion begins as early as Joseph Addison's essay in the *Spectator*, no. 419 (1 July 1712), from his series on the pleasures of the imagination, where he recommends that a poet employing the fantastic and the super-natural 'ought to be very well versed in Legends and Fables, antiquated Romances, and the Traditions of Nurses and old Women, that he may fall in with our natural Prejudices, and humour those Notions which we have imbibed in our Infancy'.

We might imagine that the transformation of superstitious belief into the supernatural sublime would involve the shedding of its associations with female story-tellers and that it would be redefined as an exclusively male preserve. This assumption lies behind the grouping by some commentators on Gothic of the works of Horace Walpole, William Beckford and Matthew Gregory Lewis as a superior class of 'horror Gothic', while the female Radcliffian school of 'explained supernatural' – in which apparently supernatural phenomena are eventually explained by natural causes – represents a lower, more timid form of 'terror Gothic'. A distinction of this kind, however, obscures the way in which all these works depend for their effect on the ability to *imagine* the marvellous, whether it be 'real' or not. Female readers were in fact among the first to express publicly their appreciation of Walpole's supernatural innovations in *The Castle of Otranto* (1764). Anna Laetitia Aikin's essay 'On the Pleasure Derived from Objects of Terror', in *Miscellaneous Pieces* (1773), represents the earliest attempt to theorize the new trend, and she may also have collaborated with her brother in producing the celebrated Gothic fragment 'Sir Bertrand' in the same volume. In 1785 the working-class poet Ann Yearsley published in *Poems on Several Occasions* a fascinating appraisal of *Otranto*. She alternately doubts her ability to express a critical opinion, as a woman and a labourer (with somewhat ironical allusion to Walpole's depiction of silly servants), and identifies passionately and presumptuously with every character in the novel, and with the author's 'magic pen' itself:

> But, oh! then strange-inventing WALPOLE guide,
> Ah! guide me thro' thy subterranean isles,
> Ope the trap-door where all thy powers reside,
> And mimic Fancy real woe beguiles.

9

The ability of a woman to embody a work of sublime genius would be triumphantly demonstrated in the same year, 1785, when Sarah Siddons first took on the role of Lady Macbeth. While she had had many previous successes, it was this role that really made her a key cultural force. Siddons *was* Lady Macbeth: 'The moment she seized the part, she identified her image with it in the minds of the living generation.'[14] And it is her unique interpretation of Lady Macbeth that held special significance for female Gothic writers, not only because of the association of the character with an atmosphere of horror and supernatural evil, but specifically because Siddons recreated the character as the main focus of the play, a charismatic figure displaying imaginative power and heroic suffering.

Siddons's own account of her first exposure to the play at the age of 20 emphasizes her imaginative engagement. Reading it alone at night, in preparation for a performance, she came to the assassination of King Duncan:

> the horrors of the scene rose to a degree that made it impossible for me to get farther. I snatched up the candle, and hurried out of the room in a paroxysm of terror. My dress was of silk, and the rustling of it, as I ascended the stairs to go to bed, seemed to my panic-struck fancy like the movement of a spectre pursuing me.[15]

From being a suggestible reader, she became an authoritative critic and explicator of Shakespeare's text. In later life she wrote 'Remarks on the Character of Lady Macbeth'. There she put forward the tendentious view that the 'fiend-like' heroine combines 'all the subjugating powers of intellect and all the charms and graces of personal beauty' which she brings to bear on the wavering Macbeth. Although 'the passion of ambition has almost obliterated all the characteristics of human nature', she is still capable of feeling genuine anguish in consequence of the crime, nobly suppressing her grief in commiseration with her husband's sufferings, but eventually succumbing to its effects, in derangement and death.[16]

These theories gave rise to some startling innovations in performance. On her first entrance she struck audiences with the simplicity of her appearance, in contrast to the formal dress and elaborate hairstyles of predecessors, preparing the way for the naturalness and psychological realism of her speech and gesture. Her variety of tone, pregnant pauses and fierce emphases, 'perfectly electrified the house',[17] and she set the pace in scenes with Macbeth down to the assassination. From the banquet scene onwards there was a decisive shift in her portrayal. She sees the ghost of Banquo as Macbeth does, and shows compassion for his distress, but stoically conceals her own feelings. Most controversial was the change she made to the sleepwalking scene. Siddons liked to recall how on her first night at Drury Lane in the role, the manager Sheridan burst into her dressing room and begged her to keep the candle in her hand throughout, as her most illustrious precursor, Mrs Pritchard, had always done. She refused, and created a sensation with her energetic miming of the lines 'What, will these hands never be clean?' Her aim was to give the strongest impression of Lady Macbeth's guilt and suffering, in order to extort pity for the murderess, and fear for her fate: 'Though pit, gallery, and boxes were crowded to suffocation, the chill of the grave seemed about you while you looked on her; – there was the hush and damp of the charnel-house at midnight; you had a feeling as if you and the medical attendant, and lady-in-waiting, were alone with her; your flesh crept and your breathing became uneasy'.[18] The overall effect was the creation of a sense of progression in the character, a fascinating complexity. The side-effect was the eclipse of Macbeth: 'every audience appeared to wonder why the tragedy proceeded further when at the final exit of Lady Macbeth its very soul was extracted'.[19] At her very last appearance at Drury Lane (naturally in her most celebrated role) the performance did indeed end with the sleepwalking scene, by audience demand.

The spectacle of Siddons's assertiveness and the knowledge of her originality in the role must have been exhilarating for all female theatre-goers. But there were elements which would have had a profound, even symbolic significance for the female writer; namely, the representation of Lady Macbeth as a woman of imagination as well as passion. All of Siddons's innovations point in this direction. It is imagination, the illusory reliving of the past, which drives Lady Macbeth to mental illness and suicide. It is imagination that allows her to see Banquo's ghost; elevated to the level of Shakespeare's greatest tragic characters, Macbeth and Hamlet, she has the vision to penetrate the invisible world. It is the highest pitch of imagination which inspires her invocation to evil spirits, asking to be possessed and unsexed, delivering herself, in Siddons's words, to 'the excitements of hell'.[20] And finally, or rather primarily, it is a leap of imagination that leads her to commit the ultimate political thought-crime, a hypothesis which will drive the action of the play: envisaging the death of the king.

For women, Lady Macbeth's act of invocation could be seen as a trope and a touchstone of the Gothic literary vocation. Siddons's reading of the passage broke powerfully with her accustomed naturalism. In a 'slow hollow whisper', her voice sounding 'quite supernatural, as in a horrible dream',[21] Siddons spoke the lines

> Come, you spirits
> That tend on mortal thoughts, unsex me here,
> And fill me from the crown to the toe, top-full
> Of direst cruelty...
> ...Come to my woman's breasts
> And take my milk for gall, you murd'ring
> ministers...
>
> (I. v. 39–42, 46–7)

It was a literal appeal for her woman's body to be possessed by infernal forces. In terms of the literary conventions of the late eighteenth century, the scene relates to the poet's demand to be possessed by divine inspiration, typical of the Ode form. In particular, it begs comparison with a developing tradition of odes addressed to the personifications 'Fear', 'Terror' or 'Horror'. In William Collins's 'Ode to Fear' (1746) – the best-known example of this type – the poet negotiates: if Fear will teach him to equal the effects of Shakespeare, then 'I, O Fear, will dwell with thee!' In this way a link was made between objects of fear or terror – natural and supernatural – and high literary ambition. Many imitations of Collins's stance followed, and women writers also laid claim to this mode of discourse. Hannah Cowley, for instance, presented her credentials as a poet of the sublime with an 'Ode to Horror' (1787). After summoning Horror 'from the *mould'ring tower,*/The *murky church-yard*, and *forsaken bower*', she announces her subjection to its power, gaining inspiration at the sacrifice of softer feelings:

Oh! bear me to th' impending cliffs,
Under whose brow the dashing skiffs
Beholds *Thee* seated on thy rocky throne;
There, 'midst the shrieking wild wind's roar,
Thy influence, HORROR, I'll adore,
And at thy magic touch, congeal to stone.

(ll. 30–36)[22]

To imagine death, to imagine violence, supernatural agency, madness, uncontrollable passion: this is the art of the Gothic writer. This is the ability women needed to lay claim to, and actively assert, in order to find success in this literary field. Like Lady Macbeth, they invoked the spirits who could lift them above the common run of sentimental conventions, unsex them, and fill them 'from the crown to the toe, top-full/Of direst cruelty'. And like Lady Macbeth, they were equally capable of expressing extremes of misery and abjection.

The celebrity of Siddons gave women a licence to explore darker and wilder themes in public writing, by setting an example of uncompromising and powerful artistry. Behind Siddons lay the authority of Shakespeare. But there were of course many other factors in play, and cultural phenomena can never be dissociated from social and political developments. Just as the Treason Trials had highlighted 'imagination' and its contagious tendency, so 'the passions', an essential element in Gothic, were an especially charged category. There were wider forces which raised the status of Shakespearian tragedy, and made Siddons the right person at the right time.

TRAFFICKING IN THE PASSIONS

There have been many different critical approaches to Gothic writing of this period. But one key element which has tended to be overlooked, no doubt because of its very obviousness, is the prominence of passion within the genre. While emotion was also an important ingredient in sentimental fiction, Gothic took its characters and readers to new extremes of feeling, through the representation of scenes and events well beyond the normal range of experience. Stage tragedy was a vital model in this respect, and Gothic emulated its effects of hyperbolic emotion.

13

Once this fundamental kinship of tragic drama and Gothic romance is acknowledged, some of the much-ridiculed 'clap-trap' of the latter mode is put in perspective. It was a rule laid down by Aristotle that tragedy was most effective when it concerned people of rank and fortune, since any decline from happiness into pain and suffering will be more notable and therefore more affecting; Gothic in its pioneering phase tended to follow this rule. More broadly, the exotic and historical settings common in tragedy were imitated in Gothic, as they seemed to justify episodes of brutal violence. They also gave greater credence to the inclusion of the supernatural, chief weapon in the arsenal of the Gothic writer for evoking the ultimate passion of terror.

The neglect of passion has been especially notable in treatments of 'Female Gothic'. While the texts are viewed as heightened representations of patriarchal society, passion appears merely as that which threatens the security and happiness of the conventionally passionless sentimental hero-ine (and by extension the author and her female readers). It is only when we bring into the picture the question of supply and demand – the dynamic nature of the texts as objects of exchange and as leisure commodities – that the *investment* of female writers and their public in passion becomes apparent. Having laid claim to visionary powers of imagination, women writers of Gothic clearly revelled in depictions of extreme and uncon-trolled emotion. Passion was their signature, their prime selling point. Ann Radcliffe *is* the impassioned villain Schedoni quite as much as the rather colourless heroine Ellena, perhaps more so: he is the product of her creative flight. Radcliffe and other Gothicists deliberately catered to the appetite for images of passion in their readers.

But what did 'passion' mean to the pioneers of Gothic and their audience? Samuel Johnson's definition in his *English Dictionary* (1755) emphasizes the plurality of meanings, and includes Locke's assertion that passion is the principle of all human activity. In today's vocabulary, 'passion' commonly has a weaker and more restricted meaning. 'Passion' has become synonymous with sexual desire, and the word is used too loosely to imply any systematic operation of feeling upon the mind or body. Almost nothing remains of the sense of danger and disapproval with which early Christianity regarded profane (as opposed to religious) emotion. The period with which we are concerned was a time of rapid secularization, which brought with it a new assessment of the nature of passion.[23] To some extent the Enlightenment, with its cult of reason, maintained the traditional suspicion of feeling. But there was an eagerness to observe with greater objectivity the influence of emotion on the minds and actions of individuals and collectivities, the better to manage emotion, or even recuperate it.

From the time of the Renaissance onwards a whole range of discourses – political, philosophical, religious, ethical, medical, economic, aesthetic – sought to give order to the world of emotion, by locating passion as an object of knowledge. This involved conceptualizing 'passion' as 'the passions', and presenting them in the form of a taxonomy, a classified schema. It was essential to discriminate between different varieties, in order to understand and control them, or ideally, subordinate them to utility. Passions are by definition irrational and unpredictable. But it was possible to sort out which passions were good and which bad, or rather, which could be channelled or sublimated into useful or beneficial ends, and which were purely negative and destructive, and must be reigned in. More subtly, it was asked which relatively harmless passions could be played against more dangerous passions, in order to neutralize them. The emerging human sciences developed an analytical terminology of emotions, discussing 'opposing passions' (such as hope and despair, delight and terror, love and hate), the 'ruling passions' and the theory of 'countervailing passions'. Two disciplines of visual interpretation were established, involving analysis of the facial features: pathognomy was the ability to discern changing emotions in the transient muscular movements of the face, and physiognomy involved the reading of governing passions in the characteristic moulding of the countenance. The purpose envisaged by such analysis might be to stabilize the body politic, to encourage religious faith, to reduce crime, to promote health, or to stimulate trade and increase national prosperity. The desire to examine and anatomize the passions was normally justified with reference to some higher political or social good.

As so often, art was a test-bed for new ideas. Charles Le Brun, painter and politician, 'the virtual dictator of the arts in France under Louis XIV',[24] wrote a treatise on the expression of the passions, which gave strict visual form to discrete emotions, laying down the law on their proper presentation. Although it was presented as a manual for artists, it was hugely influential within the wider culture, not only in France but throughout Europe. Le Brun's drawings of facial expressions became the standard iconography of externalized human nature, and their influence endured through to the early nineteenth century. Their impact is still felt in the exaggerated physiognomic descriptions so prominent in Gothic fictions. In Reynolds's portrait of Siddons as the tragic muse, the mask of Terror visible behind her throne is modelled on the image of 'Fright' from a 1734 translation of Le Brun's treatise.[25]

The imagery of Le Brun had a formative effect on eighteenth-century theatre practice, notably through the vogue for treatises on rhetoric. Works like James Burgh's *The Art of Speaking* (1763) and John Walker's *Elements of Elocution* (1781) not only described in minute detail the facial expression belonging to each distinct passion, but also prescribed the appropriate movement and arrangement of limbs. Intended as templates for acting and public speaking, they also helped to educate the audience, contributing towards an emergent demand for vivid depictions of the passions. The existence of this demand is readily apparent in the medley entertainment, *The School of Shakespeare, or Humours and Passions*, performed at the Haymarket Theatre in 1781, in which the programme took the following form:

Act I. Vanity, Henry IV, 1st part.
Act II. Parental Tenderness, Henry IV, 2nd part.
Act III. Cruelty, Merchant of Venice.
Act IV. Filial Piety, Closet-scene in Hamlet.
Act V. Ambition, Henry VIII.

Similar performances, under the same title, could be found at Drury Lane.[26]

To us this mode of representing emotion appears highly artificial. But audiences of the time were accustomed to seeing isolated feelings abstracted and displayed in conventional ways. From the Middle Ages, moral allegories such as *The Romance of the Rose* had featured personifications of the passions. In the eighteenth century the technique was still being utilized in the ode. Cowley's 'Ode to Horror', already quoted, is typical in its picturing of Melancholy who 'sits,/And weeps, and sings, and raves by fits', and Horror 'seated on thy rocky throne'. Collins's 'Ode to Fear' consists of a 'ghastly train' of such figures, including Danger '[who] stalks his round, an hideous form' and Vengeance who 'in the lurid air/Lifts her red arm, exposed and bare'. Such conventions continue to inform Gothic writing. Not only are 'sublime' poets like Shakespeare and Collins frequently quoted in Gothic fiction, but the method of representing emotion by set-piece descriptions of physiognomy, posture and movement can also be found. The project of Joanna Baillie's *Plays of the Passions* – to take a variety of emotions and write a tragedy and a comedy on each one – clearly arises from this schematic approach.

Although audiences were well versed in the conventions for representing feeling, it does not follow that they were unmoved by them. On the contrary, they were extremely susceptible to virtuoso displays. Garrick owed his reputation as an actor to his ability to communicate clearly delineated emotions; their power lay precisely in their textbook clarity. Siddons was in the same mould. One commentator described her performance in John Home's tragedy *Douglas*: 'her figure and countenance are particularly fitted to expressing the passions... her acting was the very image of fear, hope, anxiety, maternal affection and every passion which could be felt in that situation'.[27] In 1786 a book entitled *The Beauties of Mrs Siddons* appeared, which itemized in 'bold energetic language' the sensations she inspired in a variety of roles.[28] Her greatest performances were accompanied by the shrieks, convulsions, and fainting fits of those who came to marvel at her. One dazzled young female fan who saw her in York in 1796, wrote to her father: 'I am almost crazy with Dear Divine Angelic Mrs Siddons, last night is beyond every thing that ever was, or ever will be the play Isabella (Fatal Marriage I mean) you see I am cracked: her screams, two falls flat upon her face are too dreadful – as well as the madness with which she ends the play... uncle W. says he had no idea she was so great beyond all imagination he says she terrifies him out of his senses'.[29] The rhetoric of the passions was designed to produce, by sympathetic transference, exactly this kind of affect.

17

The outpouring of emotion – which might have been considered worrying – was justified to some extent by classical authority. In the *Poetics*, Aristotle had mounted a defence of the strong effects used in tragedy, by suggesting that they brought about a purgation or catharsis of irrational feelings in the viewer. There was reassurance that artificial stimulation of the passions of terror and pity would make for more moderate citizens. But nonetheless, some anxieties remained. Women's participation in the circuit of emotional exchange, for instance, was an abiding problem. The consumption of emotive images by women was problematic, partly because their more delicate nerves were thought to be at greater risk of derangement, but also because their excitement could not be sublimated into useful public activity. Instead it would fester, ruining them for domestic contentment, and at worst driving them to such desperate measures as elopement or adultery. A moral panic developed around romance fiction, giving rise to numerous strictures on female readers in periodical essays and conduct books. But it was impossible to control the proliferation of images of the passions. The traumatic scenes which had once been restricted to the supervised environment of the public theatre, were now becoming the common currency of novels which might be read alone and in secret, and the new circulating libraries made access easier than ever before. The threat of female consumption of passion could not be resolved; it could only be nullified by a change in attitudes. Gradually, through the early years of the nineteenth century, romances were reconceived as harmless escapism, unlikely to be confused with reality.

The problem of women as *producers* of powerfully emotive fictions was rather different. Here, the common wisdom was that it was an impossibility. The long-standing debate which Denis Diderot rearticulated for the eighteenth century as 'the paradox of the actor' was relevant to the issue of women as purveyors of passion. Does the actor feel what he acts? If he really feels it, can he have the presence of mind to act it; if he merely acts it, can he communicate genuine feeling? The same paradox applied to the orator, the artist, and the writer. Whichever way the decision fell, it seemed to exclude women *a priori*. Since women were barred in ordinary life from realizing the elevated passions found in tragedy, how could they voice them in art? If they did make the attempt, it must automatically be discounted as masquerade. Byron addressed the issue in characteristic terms in a letter of 2 April 1817: 'When Voltaire was asked why no woman has ever written even a tolerable tragedy? "Ah (said the Patriarch) the composition of tragedy requires *testicles*". – If this be true Lord knows what Joanna Baillie does – I suppose she borrows them'.[30] Still on the subject of testicles, a better answer was provided by the writer Germaine de Staël when, in her eagerness to meet Napoleon, she burst in upon him in his bath; 'Genius has no sex!' she declared, dismissing objections.[31]

Although evidence of female genius and mastery of the passions was confusing and inexplicable, it was sometimes acknowledged. In the case of Sarah Siddons, it was freely celebrated. 'Power was seated on her brow, passion emanated from her breast as from a shrine', William Hazlitt wrote,[32] and this verdict was echoed on every side. James Boaden said of her first performance of Lady Macbeth, 'from that hour her dominion over the passions was undisputed'.[33] An ode addressed to Siddons by Anna Seward pictures the actress enthroned and 'all our subject passions... subdued and captive there'.[34] I have already suggested that Siddons served as an inspiration for other women ambitious of fame, and that her own eminence was underwritten by the prestige of Shakespeare. But this does not fully explain how she, *as a woman*, was so willingly credited with sublime genius, normally the monopoly of men.

The clue to Siddons's success as an interpreter of the passions seems to lie in the way her own public image exemplified the dominant theory of how the passions worked. On stage she could represent emotions with a terrible veracity, to the point of frenzy and madness. But to put it bluntly, the spectators, in spite of their absorption, were secure in the knowledge of how much she was being paid for it. In other words, the violent and irrational passions she manifested were offset – in the public's eyes – by another, countervailing passion: the love of gain. This was widely acknowledged to be Siddons's ruling passion, and it happened to place her in the mainstream of contemporary philosophical and economic thinking. Cupidity was the key passion of the modern commercial state. In *The Passions and the*

Interests, Albert Hirschman has shown how early attempts to legitimate capitalism produced a theory of human nature in which covetous self-interest features in a positive, even admirable light. Montesqieu represented the acquisitive urge as a 'calm' passion which counteracted more aggressive impulses and which, by encouraging trading links, was conducive to world peace. David Hume went so far as to redefine reason itself as a passion inspired by enlightened self-interest. Greed is of course the main protagonist of Adam Smith's *Wealth of Nations*: the engine of enterprise and progress, which unconsciously brings about prosperity for all. So thorough was the recuperation of this passion, once condemned as a sin by the Christian Church, that it often went by a new name, 'interest'. The balance of passion and interest was a vital part of Siddons's public persona.

The actress's startling economic rise has been well documented. From a salary of £3 per week at the Orchard Theatre in Bath between 1778 and 1781, she went to £12 a week for her first season at Drury Lane in 1782–3, going up the next season to £20. Meanwhile her income for benefits was regularly exceeding £300. Instead of resting during the summer intermissions, she undertook exhausting tours of the provinces, at premium fees. Twelve nights in Edinburgh in May 1784 netted £967 7s 7d. In Dublin she appeared at £50 a night for twenty nights. Trouble erupted over the issue of benefits for other actors in Dublin – there were rumours that she had refused to act in a benefit for a colleague who had suffered a paralytic stroke, and had insisted on a high fee for appearing at Brereton's benefit. Meanwhile the news circulated that she'd cleared 3,000 guineas over the summer.[35] On her first reappearance at Drury Lane she was hissed and harangued until forced to leave the stage, but insisted on returning and addressing the crowd directly to justify herself. The incident became part of the Siddons legend. She was held by commentators to have shown 'astonishing firmness', 'a male dignity [of] understanding...that raised her above the helpless timidity of other women'.[36] In the aftermath, Siddons's purported first response was to abandon her career, but in the event she immediately went on to consolidate it with her first London performance of *Macbeth* in February, increased wages, and ever more profitable benefits.

The whole affair has generally been discussed as a temporary setback which left a lingering reputation for stinginess. Certainly, a 'negative' view of Siddons emerged to set beside the accolades. It is most vividly portrayed in Gillray's caricature of her (contra Reynolds's heroic portrait) as Melpomene of the money-bags (Fig. 1). The tragic muse in the person of the actress has thrown away her emblems of cup and dagger, and reaches for the loot dangling from the devil's pitchfork, though her pockets are already full to bursting with banknotes and coins. However, there are elements in the image which contradict and moderate the satire. As a portrait it is not unflattering, the theatrical pose remains graceful and dignified, and there is an elevating quality to the oval frame which Nicholas Penny takes to be a bid by Gillray for '"high art" prestige'.[37] The contradictions are telling. I want to suggest that, far from being detrimental, Siddons's covetous mystique was a positive advantage to her in helping to secure her respectability in spite of dangerously naturalistic playing of the passions. For the love of gain was a 'cool' passion, which provided an acceptable, comprehensible frame for her artistic experiments.

Siddons herself insisted that her efforts to make money were motivated by the need to secure the future of her growing family; that is, that they were dictated by moral sentiment rather than passion. But the public were unlikely to be fooled, as they read reports of spectacular profits far in excess of a comfortable maintenance. In October 1786 she wrote excitedly to friends, 'I have at last... attained the *ten thousand pounds* which I set my heart upon, and am now perfectly at ease with respect to fortune'.[38] Yet she continued to drive herself, unhindered by a miscarriage after a performance, back at work ten days after the death of her daughter, and undertaking another highly profitable tour of the provinces the next summer. (It is worth digressing to note that her relentless touring, in Scotland and Ireland as well as England meant that the culture of tragedy she helped to form was inclusively national, not simply metropolitan).

Siddons was a test-case for women wishing to traffic in the passions, and earn lots of money in the process. She showed that, in spite of the fact that neither a flair for representing sublime emotion nor sharp business-sense were considered feminine attributes, taken together they could result in a

21

Fig. 1. Sarah Siddons as 'Melpomene' by James Gillray, 1784.

respectable vocation. While original genius taken on its own was perhaps a troubling quality in a woman, lifting her above the normal run of humanity, the pursuit of profit was reassuringly far from singular. Reciprocally, signs of artistic ambition purified lucre. It was undoubtably difficult to achieve the right balance, and the writers dealt with here were not always successful in managing both their artistic and commercial reputations.

Part of initial shock-impact of Walpole's *The Castle of Otranto* and Lewis's *The Monk* was the dilettante status of the authors. They were men of rank and members of parliament. What cause could they have to portray scenes of unbridled lust and improbable violence, and stir the passions of their reader? As one reviewer wrote of the aristocratic Walpole, 'It is...more than strange that an Author, of a refined and polished genius, should be an advocate for re-establishing the barbarous super-stitions of Gothic devilism!'[39] By contrast, the women discussed in this book were made acceptable, to a greater or lesser extent, by their obvious professionalism. They had a clear pecuniary interest in attracting an audience in a sensationalist manner. The dedications and appeals to patrons which commonly introduce their narratives were a crucial part of their management of reception. They flaunted the insignia of the working author.

The following readings of the lives and works of six authors will keep in view these concerns: the legitimation of visionary imagination in women writers, methods of representing the passions, the issue of arousing the passions of the reader or audience, and the profit motive. Other central concepts will be 'original genius' and 'the sublime'; the definition and history of the terms will be explored in the course of the discussion. My approach involves special consideration of certain marginal aspects of the works, such as paratext, epigraphs, and poetic insertions in prose narrative, in addition to the usual attention to narrative technique, characterization and descriptive writing. My sense of the cultural and historical coherence of women's Gothic is based on a wider claim that Gothic writing was part of a trans-generic resurgence of tragedy towards the end of the eighteenth century. Tragedy became subject to the revisionist view that, in the words of Raymond Williams, 'both hero and spectator are conscious consumers of feeling', and their actions become 'occasions for displaying their modes of consumption'.[40]

Evidence will be developed through six case-histories of the careers of women who wrote in a variety of forms: poetry, drama and the short story as well as novels.

All of the main works I examine are available in modern editions, though not all of them are currently in print. I am grateful to the editor and publisher of the 'Writers and their Work' series for the opportunity to draw attention to a few writers still only barely admitted to literary history (alongside the better known Radcliffe and Shelley), and for enabling me to contribute in this way to the demand for new editions of works like *The Old English Baron* and *The Recess*. The best result of a book of this kind would be to help create a market for early women's writing through 'critical mass', and keep these enjoyable and historically important texts alive and circulating.

1

Clara Reeve and
Sophia Lee

FEMALE AUTHORSHIP

Clara Reeve made her literary debut in a blaze of bad temper and recrimination. *Original Poems on Several Occasions* (1769), signed C.R., opens with a dedication to the Honourable Mrs Stratford, expressing all the proper respect due to rank. But the tone changes in the 'Address to the Reader' which follows. Reeve explains that the first intention of the volume was to publish the libretti of two oratorios she had written, both on biblical subjects. She had had good hopes that the first, on Ruth, would be accepted by a composer, but halfway through a rival work on the same subject had appeared. The second, on Absolom's rebellion, was actually requested, but in this case the composer had been so dishonourable as to accept another text, and so all her labours were lost. Currently, however, it is under consideration elsewhere, which prevented her from including it here. The question was now whether to proceed with the present publication or abandon it, but on the advice of friends, she has filled up the gap with miscellaneous poems. And so it goes on. This monody is typical of Reeve's style of direct authorial address. She is at once the most confiding and defensive of writers. Too often she has been dismissed as having about her a tiresome odour of sanctity; what has been missed is the rather more piquant odour of acrimony.

Another misconception about Reeve is connected with a poem in this collection, 'To My Friend Mrs. - - - - -, on her Holding an Argument in Favour of the Natural Equality of Both the Sexes. Written in the Year 1756', namely that she was an apologist for

CLARA REEVE.

Fig. 2. Portrait of Clara Reeve, probably imaginary, from a late Victorian edition of *The Old English Baron* (London, 1883).

the subordination of women, and can therefore be considered a social conservative. This reading depends on ignoring the poem's tone of playful irony. In the poem, the shortage of women writers is traced to the qualities of the inspirational Helicon spring of Greek myth, which:

> Produces very strange effects,
> On the weak brains of our soft sex;
> Works worse vagaries in the fancy,
> Then Holland's gin, or royal Nancy.

That such statements should be taken as satirizing the prevalent view, rather than as the author's own opinion, is made apparent when she reveals that she speaks from her own bitter experience:

> Those talents that were once my pride,
> I find it requisite to hide;
> For what in man is most respected,
> In woman's form shall be rejected.
> Thus have I prov'd to demonstration,
> The fallacy of your oration.
> (You need not let the fellows know it,
> They'll praise the wit, but damn the poet.)

The opinions reviewed in fact do nothing to demonstrate the inferiority of women, but are instead exposed as nonsensical prejudice. The same theme is taken up elsewhere, most optimistically in the opening 'Address'. Reeve takes heart from the success of other female writers:

> I formerly believed, that I ought not to let myself be known for a scribbler, that my sex was an insuperable objection, that mankind in general were prejudiced against its pretensions to literary merit; but I am now convinced of the mistake, by daily examples to the contrary. I see many female writers favourably received, admitted into the rank of authors, and amply rewarded by the public...

In *Original Poems* Reeve stakes her claim as an author to be taken seriously. The very title is a gesture of self-assertion. 'Original' was a key term in the aesthetic theory of the time. Edward Young in *Conjectures on Original Composition* (1759) had influentially argued that originality and rule-breaking was the true sign of artistic value, against the neo-classical emphasis on imitation of classical models. William Duff's *An Essay on Original Genius*

(1767) helped to consolidate the trend. In reality, there is little in Reeve's poetry to justify the claim to originality (as it was regarded at the time), since, apart from the workmanlike oratorio 'Ruth', the volume mainly consists of neat satirical pieces. There is however a poem in praise of Shakespeare, and another emulating Ossian's *Fingal*, the recent literary sensation purported to be an ancient Scottish epic, which give inklings of a Gothic sensibility. Most interesting for our purposes is the opening 'Elegy' which establishes an authorial persona of acute sensibility, warm imagination and high literary ambition, subjected to perpetual misfortune.

> The laurel wreath is blasted on my brow,
> By the cold blight of disappointment chill'd,
> Disdain and Fortune have congeal'd to snow
> The ray of Genius, that my bosom fill'd.

The pose of suffering can safely be discounted as elegiac artifice. What is important is the self-proclaimed 'ray of Genius', taken in conjunction with the eight packed pages which list subscribers to the volume, including an impressive scattering of provincial gentry. Advance subscription was a favoured method of publication, with the dual advantage of guaranteeing a good income for the author, and showing that the author had an established circle of admirers. Reeve must have been well aware that her launch in the world of letters, in spite of the setbacks, was a marketing coup.

She had done well for the daughter of an obscure minister from Ipswich. Born in 1729, the eldest of eight children, she had been encouraged as a child to study history and Latin. But it seems that only after the death of her father in 1755, when she moved with her mother and two sisters to Colchester, did she seriously apply herself to literary labours. There is no evidence of financial need. Two brothers had successful careers, one becoming a vice-admiral, another a minister and master of a grammar school, and presumably they helped to support the family. After the volume of poems, Reeve's next work was a translation from Latin of a seventeenth-century romance, *Argensis* by John Barclay, published in 1772 as *The Phoenix*. It was a showy enterprise for a woman (the work is signed 'by a Lady'), and she no doubt had in mind Elizabeth Carter's prestige as a translator of Epictetus from the Greek. But already it indicates what was to be a sustained interest in the genre of romance. A few years later her response to Horace Walpole's experiment in 'modern romance', *The Castle of Otranto* (1764), resulted in her most celebrated work, *The Old English Baron*.

FRAMING THE PASSIONS

Reeve's romance was first published by a Colchester firm in 1777, anonymously and at her own expense, under the title *The Champion of Virtue: A Gothic Story*. The 'Address to the Reader' is an attempt to win a favourable reception for a type of writing consciously presented as a novelty. The *Castle of Otranto* is discussed as a flawed but admirable model. There is a transparent fiction that the text is a modernized version of a manuscript in Old English. Altogether Reeve shows a hesitancy almost equal to Walpole's when he initially peddled *Otranto* as a medieval manuscript translated from Italian, and this should be taken as sign of the still risky nature of the venture into supernatural fiction, when established canons of taste rejected all improbabilities. Happily, the first public response was favourable. In the *Monthly Review* for January 1778, the reviewer remarked:

> This writer has imitated, with tolerable success, the style and manner of ancient romance. The story is enlivened with an agreeable variety of incidents; the narrative is plain and simple; and the whole is adapted to interest the feelings of the reader, provided he has either faith, or fancy, enough to be it interested in the appearance of ghosts.[1]

Reeve acted quickly. She sold the copyright to the London publisher Dilly for £10 and in June 1778 the same reviewer noted that a second edition had appeared, revised and corrected, with a new title, *The Old English Baron*. This time the author signed her full name, but there is no comment on her sex in the review journal, beyond referring to the author as 'her'.

With success came a sense of empowerment. The Preface to the second edition has the tone of a manifesto. The criticisms of Walpole are repeated from the first edition but introduced more assertively. Reeve promotes romance as an idealizing form

29

tending to elevate manners and morals: 'The business of Romance is, first, to excite the attention; and, secondly, to direct it to some useful, or at least innocent end' (*OEB* 4). *Otranto* suggests the plan for a modernized and moralized genre of romance: it captivates readers with the marvellous, holds them with the probability of its picture of manners, and engages their feelings with its deployment of pathos. However, *Otranto* itself violates this plan by the excess of its supernatural machinery, which 'destroys the effect it is intended to excite', inviting laughter instead of wonder. *The Old English Baron* will correct this defect by keeping the story 'within the utmost *verge* of probability' while preserving its spirit of enchantment (*OEB* 4). Finally, Reeve manages to boast about the good sales of the first edition, and devotes the second edition expectantly to 'that public which has so often rewarded the efforts of those, who have endeavoured to contribute to its entertainment' (*OEB* 5). Most of the preface was reprinted as part of a review in *The Critical Review* for April 1778, giving Reeve and her contentious views maximum publicity. The critic only added that 'This is no common novel' and may 'claim a place upon the same shelf with The Castle of Otranto'.[2] It was probably via this review that Walpole learnt of Reeve's challenge. In August he wrote in a letter that the Preface is 'not at all oblique, but though mixed with high compliments, directly attacks the visionary part' of *Otranto* (letter to William Cole, 22 August 1778).

Of all the major works discussed in this book, *The Old English Baron* is perhaps the most difficult to know how to read today. Even at the time, opinion was sharply divided. Walpole, unsurprisingly, was damning in his verdict. 'Have you seen *The Old Baron* [sic], a Gothic story, professedly written in imitation of *Otranto*, but reduced to reason and probability! It is so probable, that any trial for murder at the Old Baily would make a more interesting story. Mrs Barbut's [sic] fragment was excellent. This is a *caput mortuum* [worthless residue']'[3] (letter to William Mason, 8 April 1778). Mrs Barbauld, co-author with her brother John Aikin of the 1773 fragment 'Sir Bertrand', concurred that 'we foresee the conclusion before we have reached twenty pages', and that the appeal of Reeve's supernaturalism was owing to the fact that it coincided with the beliefs of many of its readers.[4]

Yet a reviewer of one of Reeve's later productions reflected, 'When the *Old English Baron* made its appearance, every mouth was opened in its praise; every line carried fascination along with it. The younger branch of readers found their attention absolutely rivetted by the story; and at its conclusion, they have actually been seen to weep, in the spirit of Alexander, because they had not another volume to peruse. A more genuine and unaffected compliment was never paid to any work of fancy'.[5] The poet Anna Seward recorded that she read it repeatedly with pleasure.[6] There is further evidence of its wide success in a French translation of 1800, and an adaptation for the stage as *Edmund; Orphan of the Castle, a Tragedy* in the same year.

Such evidence is important. A constant concern of the present study is the issue of affect, and the precise nature of the pleasure offered to the reader in Gothic texts. It is clear from Reeve's preface that she sought to engage readers on multiple levels, through the marvellous, the probable and the sentimental. The interaction of these three levels – the narrative economy of *The Old English Baron* – can provide a model or benchmark for further investigation of the strategies of much female Gothic writing. The marvellous is connected with the strongest passions, and produces the most intense affect in the reader. It is the excess produced by the metaphysical shock of criminal actions. It is associated not only with evil, but also with the fear of death. The supernatural activates the passions concerning self-preservation which, according to Edmund Burke's theory of the sublime, are the most powerful of all the passions.[7] They serve to compel the reader's attention to the highest degree, but such feelings are intensely inward-directed, and therefore antisocial, unstable and potentially socially disruptive. Reeve's second level, the probable or the rhetoric of realism, is what makes the marvellous modern and palatable, and consequently capable of touching an enlightened, sceptical audience. Morally neutral, its function is that of a 'mixer', or a bridge between passion and sentiment. By the method of either spinning out or reducing mundane and non-affective description of actions or character, the writer can either distance or foreground emotional affect. The third level, the sentimental, facilitates the moral redemption of the passions, reorientating the narrative towards social integration. The text must 'engage the heart' through the pathetic, and this is the guarantee of the moral use-value of the novel. Representations of sentiment involve and arouse the gentler passions of pity or grief, qualified in their inwardness by the generous, outward-directed impulse of sympathy. The violence of catharsis leaves a residue of sentiment, and it is the pleasurable cultivation of sentiment which generates social cohesion through *amour-propre*: self-love, or rather, self-approval. The purely selfish passions associated with pain or danger are redeemed by softening moral sentiment, and reciprocally, compassion is made powerfully interesting by images of terror and suffering. Reeve's tripartite system of narrative is intended to create a parallel drama in the mind and heart of the reader.

In this study, as we follow the progress of women's Gothic chronologically through the texts, a general pattern emerges. The role of the admixture of probability, and the technique of filtering terror through sympathy, both become less prominent. They are reduced as other factors come into play. The passions are represented with more immediacy; less carefully framed. The Gothic mode by the 1790s is entering its proto-generic phase, and becoming recognizable as a distinct literary type. By the early 1800s it will be legitimated, if not respectable, simply by virtue of its undeniable existence. Whatever the critics and moralists thought, the literature of terror was not going to go away. Authors were able to attempt stronger and stronger effects within the bounds of now-familiar convention. At the same time, to return again to the argument of my Introduction, by the late 1780s treatment of the passions, especially by women, could be understood and justified within a 'Siddonian' frame. We will see the advent of this shift in Sophia Lee's *The Recess*. Through the 1790s, Siddons's mixed specialism in legitimate tragedy and modern Gothic drama would ensure that the thorny path of Gothic experimentation was eased by the comfort zone of a national tragic tradition.

But these developments come after *The Old English Baron*. The founding text of women's Gothic is a reading lesson, as *The Castle of Otranto* had been. Unlike *Otranto* its methods are tentative, in the knowledge that due to inexperience the reader would need only the lightest touch to resonate with the feelings depicted. One consequence is that the crime of passion which gives rise to the narrative is made not only temporally remote, but also buried within a dense structure of probability and sentiment. The author of the crime, the villain Sir Walter Lovel, is displaced both geographically and narratively. Even the titles to both first and second editions represent a displacement, since they refer to characters not immediately involved in the family drama. These various distancing devices should not be considered the result of constraints on the author, but rather as evidence of her belief in the immense affective power of the passions underlying her story.

The story begins, then, not with the usurper, not with the victims, not even with the rightful heir who has been raised as a peasant in the tradition of *Otranto*, but with a *friend* of the murdered Lord Lovel. Sir Philip Harclay is an Old English Baron, and emerges as a Champion of Virtue. He is a knight who has fought at Agincourt and is now returning to England after years of service in Greece, fighting the Saracens. After arranging his own affairs in Yorkshire (in a page or two of contingencies which establish the realism of the tale), he journeys to visit his old friend in the west of England, only to discover that he died fifteen years before (gently engaging the sentiments of the reader with this episode of attachment and loss). It is only once these filtering or cocooning layers have been put in place that a partial revelation of evil emerges through Sir Philip's 'strange and incoherent' dreams. He sees his dead friend and tries to embrace him, but cannot. He is led to a 'dark and frightful cave, where [Lord Lovel] disappeared, and in his stead he beheld a complete suit of armour stained with blood, which belonged to his friend, and he thought he heard dismal groans from beneath'. An 'invisible hand' leads him to a 'wild heath', where there are preparations for a combat, but a voice cries out that he must wait for the event when heaven allows, and he is transported back to his own home, where he finds himself happily with his friend, now living and youthful. The use of dreams as omens is designed not only to prevent confusion in navigating a new form of fantastic narration, but also to protect the feelings of the reader from being too violently aroused.

The following day, Sir Philip goes to meet the current owner of the Castle of Lovel, the benevolent Baron Fitz-Owen, related by marriage to Sir Walter, his friend's brother and heir. He is

33

struck by the manner of a young peasant-boy, Edmund Twyford, whom the baron has taken into the family as a companion for his sons and, imagining he sees a resemblance to his friend, offers to adopt him. Edmund, however, is unwilling to leave his benefactor, and Sir Philip departs, still offering his friendship in case of future trouble. Again, this is a preparation, in effect a signal, for the outburst of dangerous passions. The narration itself steps back a pace. An editorial interpellation explains that there is an interruption of four years in the tale told by the 'manuscript', and that 'What follows is in a different hand, and the character is more modern' (*OEB* 22). What follows is a series of scenes in which two young relations of the baron, Richard Wenlock and John Markham, agitate to disgrace Edmund, out of envy for his shining qualities and his position as a favourite, especially with Emma, daughter of the baron. Eventually, in a sudden shift of scene to military service in France, a fragment of text much of which is 'effaced by time and damp' describes how they conspire to murder him during a skirmish with the enemy. Edmund emerges from all the trials with added glory. These episodes play out in the present, in a moderated, even comic form, the horrific events of the past. They are traces; a rehearsal for full revelation.

The shocking truth only emerges when Edmund, back at the Castle of Lovel, agrees to spend three nights in the reputedly haunted wing of the building, shut up since the death of the previous owner and his lady. Compared with the parallel scene in *The Castle of Otranto*, Reeve's treatment is gradual. It is also, here, at its most recklessly atmospheric: 'He then took a survey of his chamber; the furniture, by long neglect, was decayed and dropping to pieces; the bed was devoured by the moths, and occupied by the rats, who had built their nests there with impunity for many generations' (*OEB* 42). Edmund attempts to explore further, when his lamp blows out leaving him in darkness; the essential Gothic trope introduced by Walpole. At the same moment a 'hollow rustling sound' is heard. For the first time fear 'struck upon his heart, and gave him a new and disagreeable sensation' (*OEB* 42). No sooner has Reeve introduced the emotion than she explains how to master it, and Edmund drops on his knees in prayer. Sustained by conscious virtue, never again will fear of the supernatural trouble him. On the third night in the haunted chambers, there is a delightful moment when he and his companions, engaged in conversation, ignore the midnight groans coming up through the floorboards: 'being somewhat familiarized to it, they were not so strongly affected' (*OEB* 69).

Effects of the uncanny are rapidly knitted into relations of sentiment. On the first night, Edmund dreams that a warrior and lady enter the room and stand by the bed where he lies sleeping. They claim him as their child and devote him to heaven and the restoration of justice. The second night, old Joseph, a former servant of Lord Lovel, tells a 'dark story' of suspected murder, also revealing Sir Walter's persecution of the widow, and the possibility of her escape as a forlorn refugee in the last stages of pregnancy. This is instantly followed by the sound of the murder being replayed in the room beneath, and the discovery of blood-stained armour. Confirmation of the crime, and of Edmund's parentage and true identity, comes when his foster-mother Margery is questioned by Edmund and his supporter, Father Oswald. At the core of her story is the chilling idea of Lady Lovel's suffering and death: having given birth, and looking for help, her foot slips and she falls into the river. Her corpse is found caught against a stake the next morning. But the affect is, as ever, mediated; in this case by the scene of story-telling which enables sentimental interjections and the dramatic framing of response.

Now assured of his identity as the true heir of the estate and title of Lovel, Edmund departs in secret to seek the support of Sir Philip Harclay, his father's friend. Back at the castle, there is a replay of his supernatural experiences as farce. The comic villains Wenlock and Markham undergo Edmund's ordeal in the haunted apartments, begin squabbling, and are ordered out by a stern ghost in armour. The main plot moves to the north of England and the Scottish border, where Sir Philip meets Sir Walter in a trial by combat and triumphs. The wounded criminal makes his confession 'in great anguish of mind' (*OEB* 103). This is the affective epicentre of the novel. Revelation of the secret of Walter Lovel's interiority, his motive, his destructive passions, is the event the narrative has laboured to anticipate and defer: 'my mind was disturbed by the baleful passion of envy; it was from that root all my bad actions sprung' (*OEB* 104). Walter envied his kinsman Arthur his grace, virtue and accomplishments, and when Arthur chose a wife and inherited a title, envy was compounded by sexual jealousy and covetousness to produce a murderous hatred. He ordered two emissaries to intercept and kill Arthur on his return from a military campaign in Wales. His corpse was brought back to the castle secretly, tied 'neck and heels' and placed in a trunk under the floorboards. Walter felt then 'the pangs of remorse' and has 'never known peace since'; he finishes by weeping as he relates that he has been punished in this world by the loss of all his children.

Reeve's management of the story from this point is especially mystifying for the modern reader. Having finally brought her tempestuous villain centre stage, she then dismisses him. The confession is his only moment of sustained self-expression. Otherwise he is for the most part a sullen cipher. Relapsing into resentment, he is glimpsed 'choked with passion': 'Lord Lovel bit his fingers, he pulled the bed clothes, he seemed almost distracted' (OEB 115); elsewhere we learn that 'he sent forth bitter sighs and groans that denoted the anguish of his heart' (OEB 121). But these displays are a mere sideshow, a reminder of why the emphasis of the plot must lie in the arduous task of legal, social and economic reparations, in what might seem an over-extended coda. With this emphasis, however, comes also a healing of the narrative. The invisible world which had burst its bounds is sealed up once more, and probability resumes its rights.

There is, however, a fleeting return to unreason and a faint echo of the pleasure of terror which Reeve has so hesitantly indulged. The gates of the Castle of Lovel spontaneously fly open to receive Edmund on his return. He and a band of 'commissioners' appointed to examine the evidence of the murder at first hand proceed to the haunted apartment. They uncover the buried trunk and open it to find the skeleton 'which appeared to have been tied neck and heels together'. A priest moralizes: 'Let this awful spectacle be a lesson to all present, that though wickedness may triumph for a season, a day of retribution will come!' (OEB 131–2). There is an illustration of this scene in the French translation of the novel, which suggests its peculiar poignancy (Frontispiece).[8] In spite of the medieval armour standing to one side, the inspectors are shown impeccably dressed in the fashions of the late 1790s; a reminder of the powerful identification of readers with the protagonists of Gothic romance, transcending the remote historical settings. They hang over the opened trunk gazing fascinatedly, even longingly, at the appalling contents – a skeleton which attracts the eye like an exclamation mark – as if to say the season of wickedness has been all too short.

The contrast of Clara Reeve's *The Old English Baron* and Sophia Lee's *The Recess; or, A Tale of Other Times* (1783–5) could not be more striking. Where Reeve handled the sublime with kid gloves, Lee's register is almost continuously histrionic. In place of Reeve's carefully regulated story-telling economy, Lee delivers a series of intimate, almost intolerably claustrophobic, confessional narratives. The main narrators, the sisters Matilda and Ellinor, are not only caught up in an incessant series of misadventures and writing from the midst of them, but we discover belatedly that their accounts are also unreliable; their fundamental motives and the perspectives arising from them cancel each other out. Their constant appeals to heaven do nothing but justify them in their headstrong careers, and whatever virtues they possess bring no happiness in this world. Passion rules in the universe of the novel. No didactic frame can contain it.

THE SIGNIFICANCE OF BATH

The author of this amoral chronicle of the lives of wayward women was the founder of a teaching establishment for young ladies in Bath. The Lee sisters turned to teaching around 1781, after the death of their father. The school was a success and provided a steady income, while also allowing Sophia and her sister Harriet time to pursue their literary ambitions. The school itself was to prove a medium for significant cultural links. It is possible that Ann Radcliffe was a pupil there; she lived with her parents in Bath from about 1774 (when she was 7 or 8) until her marriage in 1787. The writer of her obituary remarks that she was 'acquainted with Miss Lee's family' and 'among the warmest admirers of *The Recess*'.[9] Sarah Siddons also became a family friend, and sent her youngest daughter Cecilia to the school in 1799.

MISS LEE.

Fig. 3. Engraving of Sophia Lee from an original portrait by Thomas Lawrence.

The key to the apparent anomaly of Lee's dual career as pedagogue and as writer of sensational Gothic romance, lies in her theatrical background. Her father was the well known actor, John Lee. During his stormy career he had acted and quarrelled with Garrick at Drury Lane, taken his young family to Edinburgh to manage a theatre, then fallen out with his creditors and been thrown in prison, and performed for one unsuccessful season with Thomas Sheridan in Dublin. In 1778 the Lee family moved to Bath, where he took over management of the theatre, introducing Sarah Siddons, and himself acted leading Shakespearean roles, including Richard III and Macbeth. He fell ill in 1780 and died in 1781, when Sophia was 31. Where Clara Reeve began her life as a writer in frustration, Lee scored a brilliant success with her debut, the comic drama *The Chapter of Accidents*, first produced at the Haymarket Theatre in London in 1780. Even so, as in the case of Reeve, Lee's first steps in the profession showed considerable grit. She had given an early version of the play to Harris, the manager of Covent Garden, who advised her to cut it down to the length of an afterpiece. This she refused to do, and instead expanded it into a five-act comedy on the recommendation of Colman at the Haymarket. The play was acted every season until the end of the century, in over 100 performances. Loosely based on Diderot's *Le Père de famille*, romance takes second place to the circulation of money and legacies in the plot, and the moving force is economic interest. It was with the considerable proceeds from *The Chapter of Accidents* that Lee prudently invested in the school.

The start of Lee's literary career coincided with the arrival of Sarah Siddons in Bath, and the beginning of the Siddons phenomenon. The city, previously known as a seasonal magnet for the fashionable and the hedonistic, became the fulcrum of a new cultural movement: the revival of tragedy. Garrick at Drury Lane had prepared the way, but Siddons was most prominently identified with the shift in reception and taste. She arrived at the Orchard Theatre in the autumn of 1778, and played dozens of roles in the first season. Prevented from taking the main comic parts by the prior claim of another actress, her reputation was made with tragic parts, such as Elvina in Hannah More's *Percy*, Belvidera in Otway's *Venice Preserv'd*, and Lady Macbeth, which she first performed at the start of the second season.

39

'Tragedies', she remarked in her *Memoranda*, 'which had been almost banished, again resumed their proper interest... [and] were becoming more and more fashionable. This was favourable to my cast of powers.'[10] The orbit of Bath existence altered its course.

Her success changed the habits of Bath society, who had been accustomed to attending the Thursday night Cotillion Balls in the Assembly rooms. The theatre was usually vacant on those evenings, but as Sarah's attraction grew, the attendance at the balls thinned, and the fashionable began to flock to Orchard Street on Thursdays and any other night on which she acted.[11]

She quickly attracted the attention of the literati and leaders of taste, who periodically migrated *en masse* from London to take the waters. Ostensibly a retreat for invalids, Bath became a resort for the fashionable. Women dominated the scene. The Duchess of Devonshire was among Siddons's most ardent admirers and was instrumental in bringing about her triumphant return to Drury Lane. Members and associates of the bluestocking circle gathered in the city, notably Elizabeth Montagu, Hester Thrale, Anna Seward, and Frances Burney, who had achieved instant celebrity with *Evelina* in 1778. In her diary, Burney recorded a stimulating, almost feverish, programme of cultural and intellectual amusements. The mingling of art and medicine which was the medium of Bath can be seen in the provenance of *The Recess*; the novel is dedicated to Sir John Eliot, a cultivated doctor who had early recognized and encouraged Sophia's talents as a writer.

The round of pleasure and therapy was rudely interrupted in the June of 1780 by the outbreak of rioting. Lord George Gordon's petition to parliament against the Catholic Relief Act encouraged anti-Catholic protesters to take to the streets in London, attacking government institutions such as lawcourts and prisons, and the homes and businesses of Catholics and liberal sympathizers. The army and militia were called in to restore order, but around 300 people were killed (some put the number as high as 1,000), mainly as a result of arson attacks. Although the violence was concentrated in the capital, rioting spread to some provincial cities, of which Bath was the worst affected. Burney reported on the scenes to her father: 'to our utter amazement and consternation, the new Roman Catholic chapel in this town was set on fire at about nine o'clock. It is now burning with a fury that is dreadful, and the house of the priest belonging to it is in flames also. The poor persecuted man himself has I believe escaped with life, though pelted, followed, and very ill used... The rioters do their work with great composure, and though there are knots of people in every corner, all execrating the authors of such outrages, nobody dares oppose them.'[12] The Gordon Riots were described at the time as 'one of the most dreadful spectacles this country ever beheld'. They have since been described by historians as symptomatic of a 'quasi-revolutionary' situation, which also involved rebellion and war in the American colonies, a succession of invasion scares, and crises of royal and parliamentary authority.[13] Contemporary events justified a stance of historical pessimism; tragedy was undeniably the mode of the time.

Signs of this epoch of political and cultural ferment are apparent in *The Recess*. Lee sets her tale in a period of sharp conflict between Catholic and Protestant, inventing as her main protagonists the daughters of a secret marriage between Mary Queen of Scots and the Duke of Norfolk. She depicts two instances of mob violence in the context of colonial rebellion, a slave revolt in the West Indies and an uprising in Ireland. But this is not to say that the novel simply reflects the times, nor that Lee deliberately allegorizes them to make political points. Topical issues *are* raised through connotation – James Boaden remarked that Lee was probably inspired by a fierce debate over the relative merits of Mary and Elizabeth begun in Robertson's recent history of the Scottish queen[14] – but the focus of the following reading will be on the dimension of narrative performance. How are scenes of violent conflict and suffering represented to enable their pleasurable consumption by the reader?

THE NOVELIZATION OF TRAGEDY

The book was a commercial success. Lee received an extra £50 from her publisher Cadell in addition to the original payment for copyright.[15] As in the case of *The Old English Baron*, reviews of *The Recess* were largely favourable. Yet still, as in the case of the

41

earlier novel, critics noted an element of experiment in *The Recess* which put it on the borderline of acceptability. Reeve incorporated the marvellous; Lee mingled history and romance.[16] Both innovations were intended to engage the emotions of the reader more powerfully than the general run of fiction, and both, in the view of critics, threatened to interfere with the properly didactic function of the form. Reeve circumvented opposition by her narrative tact, and the provision of a self-referential reading lesson. We need to examine how, in turn, Lee succeeded in authorizing her story.

Instead of resorting to the rhetoric of the everyday, as Reeve had done, Lee stabilizes her text by employing the familiar tropes of she-tragedy. This was a genre epitomized by Nicholas Rowe's *The Fair Penitent* (1703) and *Jane Shore* (1714), which foregrounded the leading actress and allowed her to run the gamut of emotions. Lee's use of the conventions did not do away with the objection that she abused historical fact by confusing it with romance, but it gave the resulting blend an impressive aesthetic plausibility. The characters of Matilda and Ellinor in *The Recess* are both parts written, in effect, for Siddons. Alternately they 'take the stage', and perform there an astonishing series of 'galvanizations', set-piece embodiments of the passions, sometimes unitary (crushing grief, overwhelming horror), sometimes combined like a virtuoso fireworks display.[17] Siddons as Calista in *The Fair Penitent* apparently succeeded in communicating 'the mingled passions of pride, fear, anger, and conscious guilt'. Lee's Matilda similarly describes how 'Grief, anger, shame, and horror, divided and tore me in pieces' (*R.* iii. 270). But there are also important differences in the way the operations of identification and transference of emotion between character and audience takes place in the theatre and in fiction, which will be made apparent by briefly examining a she-tragedy Sophia Lee actually wrote as a vehicle for Siddons, *Almeyda, Queen of Granada*.

The play opened at Drury Lane on 20 April 1796. It continued for only five nights, and was not revived, but the author was nevertheless pleased with the result. In the version published by Cadell and Davies the same year, which Lee dedicated to Siddons, she thanks the public for the 'tears with which it has been honoured', and expresses her pleasure at having been 'the means of displaying, in a new point of view, [Mrs Siddons's] various powers'. The play is set in Spain under Moorish rule, where Almeyda is torn by her love for a Christian prince and the demands of her royal inheritance. It is a situation further complicated by the ambitions of her wicked uncle, Abdallah, but the heroine's chief enemy is her own nature:

> She is too frank, incautious, and ungoverned.
> More rude than cataracts her passions rage...
> She must *conceal* those passions to be *great*,
> *Subdue* them to be *happy*...[18]

The emotional highpoint comes in the first scene of Act IV, which begins when the curtains draw back to reveal a spectacular tableau: the hero Alonzo is found chained to a pillar in 'A dark vault irregularly hewn in the rock, extending out of sight on one side, in a vista of rude imperfect pillars'.[19] In this place of 'murky horror' beneath the castle, the villain disposes of his victims. Abdallah attempts to torture the captive Alonzo with a description of his fate, and, in a further *coup de théâtre*, orders a boulder to be raised by levers, to reveal a deep chasm ending in an underground river. Miraculously Alonzo escapes, but when Almeyda arrives moments later to find the prison empty she imagines he has been murdered, and becomes distracted, the background noise of rushing water mimicking her torrential passions. There is a lengthy mad scene – Siddons's forte – and only the intervention of a sympathetic guard prevents her from throwing herself into the gulf.

All the evidence of reception suggests that set-piece scenes such as this worked viscerally on the audience. They were savoured as autonomous spectacles, out of any context of plot development. The visual effect of the stage set and the violent body language of the actors are the essential means of conveying emotion. In textual terms, the method is intensive: situations and personalities are established rapidly in broad strokes. As Lee remarked in the 'Advertisement' to the published play, the theatre requires 'compression and brevity'. The method of *The Recess* is very different, as its expansive three-volume length testifies, in spite of striking similarities of theme and characterization. Replacing instant visual shock, her novel involves extensive development of motives, personalities, chains of cause and effect: the precondition of emotional transference between character and reader at the point of crisis. In order for the feelings of characters to be *felt* they must be fully *understood*. The result in *The Recess* is tragedy as autobiography, a mode which is anything but compressed. While the memoir form was not itself new to fiction, Lee's innovation lies in employing it primarily as a showcase and medium for the passions. Mary Shelley, as we will see, was a successor.

The narrative is couched in the form of a memoir intended for a sympathetic female friend by the dying Matilda, which encloses a number of other documents, including a diary kept by Ellinor and addressed to her absent sister, a number of letters written by Ellinor to her friend Lady Pembroke, and some notes by Lady Pembroke. It is the affection of the friend, Adelaide, that draws the story out of Matilda; the story-teller claims that she would prefer to leave no trace of her sufferings, but concedes that 'consummate misery has a moral use', and that 'if these sheets reach the publick' they might teach those who have suffered lesser sorrows not to repine (*R*. i. 2). Not a particularly persuasive didactic justification, given the fantastical nature of the novel's events.

It is with fantasy that Matilda begins, as she evokes her mysterious upbringing, with Ellinor, in the Recess. The reader is plunged into this strange world without bearings, prompting from the start imagination, curiosity and wonder. We are told *what* the Recess was – an underground series of man-made rooms linked by passages and staircases, into which the sun only dimly penetrates through painted glass casements – but not *where* or *why*. We are introduced to the inhabitants, the young sisters, a kind and gentle woman they call 'mamma', a maid, and a priest, without knowing who they are. In this, we are at one with the two girls themselves, who ask questions without receiving answers and wander the Recess looking for clues. Eventually they emerge into the daylight, but only to spend three years in almost equal seclusion in the nearby home of their protector's brother, Lord Scroope. An emergency causes them to return to the Recess, and the ailing woman finally dissolves the mystery.

We learn that the Recess was created as a place of retreat when a young woman discovered that the man she loved and had just married was her brother. They part, and separately retire from the world. Some years later, the woman, Mrs Marlow, becomes the guardian and mentor of the twin daughters of Queen Mary and takes them into her hiding place, to protect them from the ill will of Queen Elizabeth. They are joined by her brother, known as Father Anthony, now devoted to piety. The function of the Recess in relation to the narrative now also becomes apparent. The origin of the Recess lies in the prohibition of romantic passion, and it has come to serve as a shelter from criminal passion. It is space reserved for the development of the tender affections exemplified by Mrs Marlow. But if any lesson is taught, it is that the attempt to guard against the passions is the guarantee of their eventual ascendancy. All Father Anthony's admonitions in favour of retirement and against the evils of the world, merely foster in Matilda and Ellinor the desire for escape. He himself becomes food for their restless imaginations during childhood. Ellinor sees him as a cannibal magician in the service of a giant who holds them prey; Matilda, more charitably, as the 'guardian genius' of a circle of safety (R. i. 6). As young women, after the death of Mrs Marlow has severed their emotional attachment to the Recess, and possessed of their identities, their appetite for experience becomes more voracious than ever. Disregarding their protector's dying words to show patience if they are to achieve happiness and a restoration of their rights, the girls find an escape route and make secret sorties into the outside world. An accidental meeting with the refugee Leicester launches the narrative proper.

Matilda's love for Leicester, and their union in marriage, bring both young women into a second world, almost as strange as the first, though this time the names of historical personages and real places provide a delusory sense of recognition. It is a world without fathers, real or symbolic. Father Anthony, who had appeared a 'gloomy tyrant' (R. i. 83), had in fact been powerless to prevent Matilda's wishes; he prefigures a long succession of men whose pretended authority conceals weak and vacillating natures, which make them contemptible. It is a world ruled by women, in which women in turn are ruled by their passions, and history is therefore driven by the passions of women. There is an encyclopaedic display of emotions: Queen Elizabeth motivated by pride, infatuation and vengeance; Mary Queen of Scots prey to misdirected romantic passion; Lady Mortimer and her religious enthusiasm; the jealousy of the mutable Miss Walsingham, rival first of Matilda and then of Ellinor, who becomes Lady Sidney then Lady Essex; and finally the vindictive and murderous Lady Somerset. Matilda and Ellinor are no different; like their mother they shift between the ruling passions of romantic passion and ambition, and bring the men who love them to destruction. Leicester and Essex are themselves the slaves of Elizabeth's changing moods, sex-objects rather than self-determining subjects. It is in this world-turned-upside-down that rape becomes a ubiquitous threat. Almost every man that Matilda or Ellinor encounters wishes to 'marry' them (in a transparent euphemism), or to staightforwardly ravish them. Lee's version of Elizabethan England accords with Freud's theory of the tribe; it is the existence of a dominant male that prevents sexual anarchy.

From the meeting of Matilda and Leicester, the story becomes a tragedy. The sisters are irresistibly drawn into the vortex of evil, the court of Elizabeth, and variously banished to spend years in miserable imprisonment, before witnessing the destruction of their loved ones. The question of how the reader, alongside the protagonists, can withstand this barrage of misery, is raised self-consciously in Matilda's response to the murder of her adored Leicester. Her first answer is that the brief moments of peace and happiness which allow softer sentiments to flourish, give strength: 'These sacred pauses in life, which lovers only know, invigorate the soul as sleep does the body, and alone can enable us to sustain the past and coming ills' (R. ii. 47). But the suggestion is also made that continuous misfortune strengthens the nerves and makes the victim almost indestructible:

> You will be astonished, madam, at my surviving such unceasing and complicated misfortunes, and, above all, the loss of my beloved. I regard it myself with wonder, and impute my strength both of body and mind solely to the knowing no pause in my sufferings. Driven from one fatigue to another, lamentation was continually suspended either by amazement, or that necessity for exertion which gives a spring to all but the weakest minds, and counteracts despondency. Grief, I may affirm from sad experience, cannot be fatal till it stills and condenses every other passion. (R. ii. 76–7)

In fact the conduct of the narrative is determined by a policy somewhere in between relief through intermissions of sentiment, and nonstop emotional endurance test. Subtle discriminations in the treatment of passion are made through the dual histories of the two sisters. Although they are to some extent 'twins in misfortune', one born an hour before the other, their fortunes separate them towards the close of the first volume, and they are never truly reunited.

When Matilda discovers she is pregnant, it precipitates a crisis leading to her flight to France and a whole train of disasters: the death of Leicester, her abduction and transportation to Jamaica, and imprisonment with her daughter Mary for eight years, before returning to Britain. In the meantime Ellinor is abandoned to the wrath of Elizabeth, is made to feel responsible for the execution of her mother, Queen Mary, and endures further torments resulting from a clandestine romance with the Earl of Essex and a forced marriage to the selfish courtier Lord Arlington. She becomes prey to bouts of madness due to guilt at her mother's death and frustrated love for Essex, and by the time of Matilda's return has descended into an irreversible alienation of mind.

Ellinor, in her version of their lives, speaks of 'the appointed moment, when the paths of life, in which we have hitherto trod hand in hand, begin to separate; and every succeeding step bears us farther from each other, till darkness and distance rob the straining eye of its first dear object... while the impetuous passions drag us irresistibly onward' (R. ii. 166). 'Darkness and distance': the haunting phrase would be used again, uncannily or allusively, by Mary Shelley in the last line of Frankenstein, at the parting of the dying creator and his monster. As in Frankenstein, the autobiography of one protagonist is cradled in that of the other; given their closeness, the differences in the two accounts tend to make the reader's interpretation of events problematic. Matilda's would seem to be the dominant voice; it is she who directly addresses posterity. Ellinor's history is a fragment, incorporated within Matilda's narrative. The hierarchy of voices apparently gives precedence to moral sentiment over passion. Matilda, although capable of showing great strength of mind, is the more conventional character. For her, adversity has been softened by loving relations with her husband and daughter. From the start, Ellinor is acknowledged by her sister to have a more vivid imagination. In her own account, she emerges as a figure of extraordinary impetuosity and daring. For a while she sublimates her passion for Essex in heroic attachment to duty and a vicarious investment in his military career. But eventually she comes to believe that the harassment of her husband gives her a licence for adultery, and she dresses as a man to escape to war-torn Ireland and join Essex. Eventually she plots with him to overthrow Elizabeth, and it is the discovery of the conspiracy and his execution that drives her to madness. If Ellinor is made the passionate core of the novel, it would appear that Matilda is the stabilizing frame.

But does Matilda's retrospect make moral judgement possible? Not really. As a girl, she had said to the dying Mrs Marlow 'from your eye alone have we learnt when we did any thing aright; we shall no longer know good from evil when that dear eye is closed' (R. i. 24). The advice to preserve the 'small still voice' of conscience from being drowned out by 'the noise of the world' has never been heeded by Matilda or Ellinor. The narrative as a whole adheres to no coherent system of value. There is, for instance, no consistent moral differentiation of Protestant from Catholic. The revolts of the slaves in Jamaica and of the Irish against their British overlords are neither praised nor blamed. Both Matilda and Ellinor attempt to explain and validate their conduct by reference to the intrinsic worth of the men they love. But in addition to their own obliquely expressed doubts, in each case the investment of one is undermined by the other: Ellinor ferociously attacks the integrity of Leicester; while Matilda conveys hints of the short-comings of Essex. The final section does not bring reassuring closure. Matilda has learnt nothing from her experiences, and harbours perilous dynastic ambitions for her daughter Mary which will lead to the latter's abduction and death. The description of Matilda's first response to her loss is a powerfully effective contrast to the ceaseless torrent of emotion: 'A still agony, more dreadful than the wildest tumults of the passions, numbed my very soul' (R. iii. 312). The discourse, like her life, is near its end. Yet still she has the strength to resist an attendant priest's orders to 'controul your passions' (R. iii. 347), forget the past, and elevate all thoughts to God, and instead embarks on the act of recollection which constitutes the novel. Passion has wiped out every human tie belonging to the narrator, like the plague in Mary Shelley's *The Last Man*, but she is determined to keep the tale of passion circulating, unredeemed, and with undiminished affect for the reader. It is enough that she has survived the wreckage, a solitary witness.

*

After the publication of these two strange and adventurous works, *The Old English Baron* and *The Recess*, Reeve and Lee both appear to have suffered a loss of confidence. Since there was no sense at the time of the Gothic genre as an established mode, it was not obvious that success with a tale of supernaturalism or mental extremes was anything more than a one-off. Reeve relates that she hesitated over her next step until encouraged by friends to attempt another ghost story, 'since it seems to be my bent'. The resulting work – entitled 'Castle Connor; an Irish Tale' – was lost on the Ipswich to London coach on the way to the publisher. Reeve was later (in the Preface to *The Exiles*) to issue dire warnings should it ever appear in pirated form. It is in fact possible that the missing text reappeared as a tale of the explained supernatural set in Ireland, part of a much later novel, *Fatherless Fanny*, which was printed in Sheffield in 1816, ten years after her death.[20] The Preface to this novel is a scrambled version of the Preface to *The Old English Baron*, and indicates an unscrupulous editor with designs to exploit Reeve's reputation. Reeve next published a domestic fiction, *The Two Mentors* (1783), and a significant work of criticism, *The Progress of Romance* (1785), which asserted the value of the novel form and of a woman's perspective in the world of letters. She returned to fiction and darker territory with *The Exiles; or Memoirs of Count de Cronstadt* (1788). Around the same time, Sophia Lee published her next work after *The Recess*, *Warbeck* (1786). Both *Warbeck* and *The Exiles* were adaptations of narratives by the French author Baculard D'Arnaud; the stories 'Varbeck' and 'Le Comte de Gleichen' from *Nouvelles Historiques* (1776). D'Arnaud was noted for the harrowing effect of his tales of sensibility, and they were invariably toned down by translators for the English audience.

Lee and Reeve were more intrepid than most – *Warbeck* for instance includes a scene in which a mother protecting her child is stabbed to death – but still the resort to the relative safety of the translation business represents something of a retreat. In the 1790s, as we have seen, Lee made another bid for literary distinction with *Almeyda*; while her sister Harriet made notable contributions to the development of Gothic with the play *The Mysterious Marriage* (1798) and the short story 'Kruitzner' published in their joint volumes entitled *Canterbury Tales* (1797–1805). In 1793 Reeve published *Memoirs of Sir Roger de Clarendon*, a romance set in the fourteenth century which in its careful historicism resembles Ann Radcliffe's final novel, *Gaston de Blondeville*.

Radcliffe was the first woman writer to make 'Gothic' elements – both supernaturalism and the preoccupation with the passions – the exclusive focus of her career. And she did so with such pre-eminent success that she incidentally established Gothic as a recognizable literary mode.

2

Ann Radcliffe

Radcliffe's heroines are women of imagination. By their taste for
scenery and aptitude for fancy they transform the plots of
sentimental fiction into otherworldly romance: they are effectively the co-authors of their own stories. Their risky adventures
give them every opportunity to display their 'genius', and they
are amply rewarded in the end. In this manner, Radcliffe
repeatedly allegorizes her own triumphant career as a writer.
She was the 'Queen of the *tremendous*', 'the Shakspeare of
Romance Writers'.[1] One review, possibly by Mary Wollstonecraft, said of her, 'the spell, by which we are led, again and
again, round the same magic circle, is the spell of genius'.[2] As
Michel Foucault has observed, she has the rare distinction of
figuring as the 'founder of a discursive practice'.[3] It was a
phenomenon frequently noted at the time. A multitude of
Gothic novels by lesser writers were categorized by the critics as
belonging to the 'Radcliffe school'. 'Radcliffe' connoted an
immediately recognizable style of lyrical prose writing, playfully
invoked by Keats in a letter to a friend: 'I am going among
Scenery whence I intend to tip you the Damosel Radcliffe – I'll
cavern you, and grotto you, and waterfall you, and wood you,
and water you, and immense-rock you, and tremendous-sound
you, and solitude you'.[4] 'Radcliffe' became the name for a
particular narrativized relation to the world. One would, like
Washington Irving on a tour of Europe, see a castle through the
window of the coach, and instantly a web of Radcliffean
romance would be woven around it in the mind of the viewer.[5]

It is strange, given her celebrity and influence, that Radcliffe is
the only author discussed in this book of whom, apparently, no
portrait exists. But she shunned personal disclosure. It is usual
to preface a biographical account of her by stating that little is

known. Notoriously, in the 1880s, the poet Christina Rossetti abandoned an attempt to write her life through lack of material. But today, thanks to the painstaking efforts of Deborah Rogers and Ricter Norton, much more has come to light about her early life and family circumstances, her husband the newspaper proprietor William Radcliffe, and the period after she abandoned her publishing career in 1797.[6] She was born Ann Ward in London in 1764. Her background was humble – her father owned a haberdasher's shop and seems often to have been in financial difficulties – but it was also culturally rich. She spent much time during her early youth in the home of her maternal aunt, whose husband, Thomas Bentley, was a partner in the fashionable Wedgwood chinaware firm. By this means she came into contact with some of the prominent figures of the day, including the female authors Hester Thrale, Elizabeth Montagu and Anna Laetitia Barbauld. She also benefited from her residence in Bath from the age of 7 or 8 until her marriage. The generative nature of Bath society in this period has been described in the previous chapter: the rise of Siddons, the presence of the bluestockings, the circulation of metropolitan ideas and tastes, the shock of the Gordon Riots, the example of Sophia Lee's experiments with historical romance.

In 1787 she married William Radcliffe, an Oxford graduate trained in law, and they moved to London. He soon became editor and later the owner of a newspaper. The *English Chronicle* was a liberal publication, associated with the opposition Whig party and, like other newspapers, often published new poetry. This would have been another way in which Ann kept abreast of the political and cultural currents of the day. The Radcliffes had no children, but appear to have been a devoted couple. They made many tours together, and co-wrote an account of their trip to the Continent in 1794. Ann died in 1823, possibly of an asthma attack, after a long period of ill health. In 1826 her final novel, *Gaston de Blondeville*, was published with a 'Memoir of the Life and Writings of Mrs Radcliffe' by Thomas Noon Talfourd, based on information supplied by William Radcliffe, and this has been the chief source for all later accounts of her life. Radcliffe's publishing career lasted from 1789 to 1797, short but quite prolific: five novels including a good number of poems, and a travel journal. Later she wrote another novel, *Gaston de*

Blondeville, or The Court of Henry III Keeping Festival in Ardenne and a long narrative poem, *St Alban's Abbey*, both published posthumously. There is a tradition, beginning with Talfourd's memoir, which has it that she came to writing as a bored housewife. While there may be some truth in it, the story belies the obvious signs of her professionalism – her steady output, each work increasing in length or complexity, her willingness (after critical acceptance) to use her own name, her escalating income. Even her concealment of any details about her private life might be understood as a canny strategy to enhance her authorial mystique. Above all, this myth of the retiring, accidental authoress is denied by the evidence of high artistic ambition in the texts themselves. If we look at Radcliffe's *oeuvre* in the context of the general run of fiction at the time, we can see her impatience with the condescending approval of the reviewers for safely 'improving' fiction. In each work she showed a determination to startle them into a different and more respectful response. What's more, she succeeded. After the short notices received by the early works of her apprentice- ship, each of her new productions became literary events. They were granted the dignity of review articles, generally rapturous in their praise. Before Scott, and in a very different way, Radcliffe was attempting to place fiction on a new footing within the hierarchy of genres. The 'Gothic Stories' of Walpole and Reeve, and Lee's overwrought emotionalism, had revealed a potential which Radcliffe was determined to pursue and capitalize on: that of the novelist as visionary.

Nathan Drake's crowning epithet for Radcliffe, the Shake- speare of Romance, was not simply the hyperbole of a fan. It was an appropriate response to the author's calculated design. It refers to her daring efforts to place her work in direct line of succession from Shakespeare and Milton through the pre- Romantic poets, James Thomson, William Collins, Thomas Gray, James Beattie. Radcliffe's usurpation was carried out by a variety of means which will be examined, but most obviously through the tried and tested method of quotation, and a form of textual kidnapping quite new to the novel: the epigraph. Just as the cultural authority and professional success of Sarah Siddons rested on Shakespeare and the tragic tradition, so Radcliffe, who had witnessed at first hand the apotheosis of Siddons, raised her literary claims on the basis of Shakespeare and the tradition of the sublime, incorporating within her fictions both tragic drama and lyric poetry.

LITERARY BANDITRY

Bandits, or rather *banditti*, to use the Italian coinage the novelists preferred, are a vital element of Gothic writing. They appear in two notable forms. First there is the anonymous rabble of low-life villains, chiefly interesting for the threat to life they pose. Such are the forest outlaws of Smollet's *Ferdinand Count Fathom* or Lewis's *The Monk*. The other type, regenerated for the modern era by Schiller's drama *The Robbers*, involves a leader who has fallen from high rank through terrible misfortune and who, although he engages in the criminal trade of plunder and kidnapping, retains the marks of nobility in his character. Translated to Britain, this figure recalled Milton's Satan, and is found in William Godwin's *Caleb Williams*, Charlotte Dacre's *Zofloya*, and Byron's *The Corsair*.

Radcliffe's *banditti* are always of the first, anonymous, type. In *A Sicilian Romance* and *The Mysteries of Udolpho*, their narrative function is to disrupt the plans of the main protagonists, and create new complications in the plot. They also contribute an atmosphere of lurking doom, equivalent to their presence in the landscape paintings of the Italian baroque artist Salvator Rosa, whom Radcliffe greatly admired. The second type, the fallen prince, appears however, performatively, in the intertext of Radcliffe's novels. The epigraphs and casual quotations from established literature of the sublime is the mark of Radcliffe's 'inner worth' as a writer. Even as she traffics in the critically 'illegal' excesses and improbabilities of romance fiction, she creates an authorial persona of the noble outsider in a fallen world of commodified literary production through her display of cultivated sensibility, her dramatized admiration for her 'kidnapped' texts from Shakespeare, Milton and company.

Radcliffe's earliest use of the technique is cautious. The title page of her first novel, *The Castles of Athlin and Dunbayne* (1789), bears an epigraph from the poem 'Abelard to Eloisa' by James Cawthorn, a mid-eighteenth-century writer with a modest reputation. The use of quotations on the title page of works of fiction was already a common practice, and in this case the choice was justified by its promise of a moral lesson, in the style of *The Old English Baron*:

> – for justice bares the arm of God,
> and the grasp'd vengeance only waits his nod.

It anticipates the familiar plot of usurpation: the peasant discovered to be a prince. Elsewhere Osbert, Earl of Athlin, the peasant's friend and mentor, is referred to knowingly as 'the champion of virtue' (*CAD* 35), title of the first edition of Reeve's Gothic story.

The epigraph on the title page of *A Sicilian Romance* (1790), shows Radcliffe's developing confidence. She takes an evocative fragment from *Hamlet*, 'I could a tale unfold . . .', the words of the murdered King Hamlet to his son, which if the complete passage were restored would beautifully prepare Radcliffe's reader for the delightful terrors in store:

> But that I am forbid
> To tell the secrets of my prison-house
> I could a tale unfold whose lightest word
> Would harrow up thy soul, freeze thy young blood
> Make thy two eyes like stars start from their spheres,
> Thy knotted and combined locks to part,
> And each particular hair to stand on end
> Like quills upon the fretful porcupine.

(I. v. 13–20)

Quite a promise. Alison Milbank in her edition of the novel has indicated the semantic value of the Hamlet reference: it is a compact but highly effective preliminary for a tale of terror which concerns imprisonment and a murder mystery. Its performative value is more complex. First of all, the initiating allusion to Shakespeare indicates the transposition of tragic themes, characters and effects to the novel, a process already described in Sophia Lee's work. In addition, by this quotation, Radcliffe the author assumes the voice of the ghost, identifies herself as narrator with his metaphysical powers, and implicitly draws attention to the strange status of the epigraph as a species of utterance. The voice of the absent, the dead, located in the no man's land which surrounds the narrative.

After *A Sicilian Romance*, the deluge. Not content with the title page, Radcliffe begins to colonize new areas of the text for her epigraphs, at the start of each chapter. *The Romance of the Forest* (1791) is headed by a quotation from *Macbeth*, and other lines from the same play are used on the title pages of each volume of the first and second editions. Within this frame, there are chapter epigraphs from a range of dramas, mainly tragedy: *As You Like It* (for its forest setting), *Julius Caesar*, *King Lear*, *King John*, and more *Macbeth*; Horace Walpole's Gothic play *The Mysterious Mother* (an avant-garde choice, since it was considered that its incest plot made it too obscene to perform); William Mason's fashionable tragedies modelled on ancient Greek precedent, *Caractacus* and *Elfrida*. Her poetic sources are Thomas Warton's 'The Suicide' (twice), William Collins's 'Ode to Fear' (twice), 'The Passions, An Ode for Music', and 'Ode to a Lady on the Death of Colonel Ross in the Action of Fontenoy', James Beattie's *The Minstrel* (three times), Joseph Trapp the Younger's 'Virgil's Tomb', Anna Seward's 'Monody on Major André', James Thomson's 'Winter' from *The Seasons*, Thomas Gray's 'The Bard', and... herself. Like Alfred Hitchcock, she made a habit of popping up in cameo appearances in her own work. Those epigraphs unprovided with the usual attribution have also been untraceable by the modern editors, and we can assume that Radcliffe was here playfully leaving the cryptic signature of the *auteur*. Apart from this eccentricity, the catalogue of poets reads for the most part like a who's who of the emerging canon of sublime poetry (rather different from our retrospective canon). Here, the ode, which along with tragedy is the poetic genre most closely associated with the expression of the passions, predominates.

The same names and titles constantly appear in *The Mysteries of Udolpho* (1794) and *The Italian* (1797), with a few notable alterations. In keeping with the mood of melancholy and dreamy reverie that prevails through long sections of *Udolpho*, Radcliffe extended the scope of her literary plundering to include James Thomson in new and softer aspects – other parts of *The Seasons*, *The Castle of Indolence*, 'Hymn on Solitude' – and, for the first time in the epigraphs, Milton: *Comus* and *Il Penseroso*. Shakespeare still dominates, but in addition to the presence of his most blood-curdling tragedies, there are extracts from *A*

Midsummer Night's Dream, *Antony and Cleopatra* and *Romeo and Juliet*. Frank Sayers's tragedy *Moina* is used twice. In *Udolpho*, to a greater extent than in her other works, quotations are densely interwoven in the text of the narrative. Lines and phrases from Thomson and Milton abound, as if Radcliffe were attempting to demonstrate her mystic possession by them. Her meandering fiction seems to evolve spontaneously out of the words and ideas of great poets. At the same time, Radcliffe shows ambitions as an arbiter of taste: among the writers quoted incidentally in the text are two contemporary female authors, Charlotte Smith and Hannah More. Smith's narrative poem *The Emigrants*, which is cited, had appeared only the year before while Radcliffe was in the process of writing *Udolpho*.

The Italian keeps to the same standard repertoire: eleven epigraphs from Shakespeare (a broad range of tragedies and a few comedies), four from Milton, and a scattering of more recent poets and dramatists, among whom Horace Walpole is notable. There are three extracts from *The Mysterious Mother*, including the key epigraph at the head of the first chapter: 'What is this secret sin; this untold tale,/That art cannot extract, nor penance cleanse?' The prominence of Walpole's play has a number of consequences. First, it could suggest that Radcliffe was conscious of a link between her writing and his; not necessarily an independent 'Gothic' tradition as yet, but perhaps a sense of their joint debt to Shakespeare in the attempt to challenge realist and sentimental conventions. At the same time, the reference is sensationalist and titillating; it implies that the story will hinge on a crime at least equivalent in its horror to incest.

What effect in general did Radcliffe's literary kleptomania and name-dropping propensities have on her status as an author? I have suggested that by this method she succeeded in bolstering her credentials as a writer to be taken seriously, with powers that aspired towards the standards set by the great national poets. To read a Radcliffe novel was not simply to idle away a few hours on a silly story. Her most celebrated works were freighted with a massive accumulation of cultural capital. The effect of the strategy can be measured in column inches. *Athlin and Dunbayne* and *A Sicilian Romance* received the brief notices customary for novels. *The Romance of the Forest* achieved a breakthrough with a five-page review article in the *Monthly*

Review. *Udolpho* was a phenomenon: five pages in the *English Review*, six in the *Analytical Review* and the *Monthly Review*, seven in the *European Magazine*, eleven pages in the *British Critic* and the same in the *Critical Review*. For *The Italian* the impact was reduced, but reviews were rarely less than five pages in the major periodicals. Reviewers seldom commented on the epigraphs and quotations from the literature of genius, but they used them as the criterion by which to judge the work of Radcliffe, when praising her originality, her poetic prose style, the irresistible spell she cast over the reader.

For all its evident success, Radcliffe's device brought with it some difficulties of reception. While critics were willing to treat her novels as works far above the common run of popular fiction, they were nonetheless novels, designed to attract a broad audience. The author's narrative method lay in combining disparate elements: lyrical poetry, detailed landscape description, and a riveting plot dependent on apprehension and suspense. There were mutterings rising to widespread complaint in the periodicals that the poetic and descriptive parts interrupted the pleasure of the plot, and further that, once the mysteries on which the plot revolved were dispelled by a first reading, the value of the whole became redundant. These arguments are interesting as a sign of the novelty of Radcliffe's approach and the disruption of expectations her work provoked. At one level the problem is connected with the growing stratification of high and low literature: are the novels disposable entertainment or enduring works of art? At another level, they present a real problem of reading competence. Although there is plenty of evidence that her fictions were read and reread with great enjoyment at the time, to read the work *in full* would require an acrobatic flexibility of attention. The gratifications offered by a sonnet on evening, a prose picture of the Apennines, and the dispersal of the enigma of what lies behind the black veil, are entirely unlike. The possession of these heterogeneous pleasures takes place within different temporalities of reading, and necessitates different modes of 'literacy'. Jane Austen's Henry Tilney may have read *Udolpho* 'in two days – with his hair standing on end all the time',[7] but it is unlikely that his reading involved a thorough digestion of the eighteen poems in the book, or appreciation of the aptness of the many short poetic citations. The epigraphs, with their oblique relation to the narrative, will fall the first victims to the compulsive plot. Yet, as I hope I have shown, they were a vital part of Radcliffe's art, and of her standing in the literary world.

These ambiguities are best explored through a more detailed examination of the texts. It is clear that Radcliffe herself was aware of the difficulties and sought to remedy them from one work to the next. The very obvious change of direction, in *The Italian* especially, shows she had taken account of the critics' objections to the excess of poetry and description, which rose to a crescendo with *Udolpho*. Nevertheless, she never abandoned the commitment to imagination. She continued her attempts to integrate plot and poetry, popular appeal and genius, and in this aim the figure of the heroine – both a narrative actor and a repository of aesthetic value – was central.

THE REDEMPTIVE POWERS OF FEMALE GENIUS

A Sicilian Romance, Radcliffe's second novel, begins with a framing device: the narrator is a traveller visiting Sicily, who comes across the ruins of the house of Mazzini, and is impressed by the picturesque situation and 'air of grandeur'. Its abandoned state provokes reflections on mortality, but it also suggests an enigma, arousing 'awe and curiosity'. A passing friar points to the ruin: 'These walls ... were once the seat of luxury and vice. They exhibited a singular instance of the retribution of Heaven, and were from that period forsaken, and abandoned to decay.' He arranges for the traveller to see a manuscript which recounts the history of the castle, and from this manuscript the text of the novel is said to derive.

The brief episode epitomizes Radcliffe's preferred narrative method. Uncanny phenomena exist in the present as signs and relics of a primordial crime. The castle ruins are uncanny in the strict sense: un-homelike, alienated, mystifying. At the same time they are curiously human, like a face that has been furrowed and eroded by a lifetime of strong emotion. They speak to the viewer, communicating the promise of the title-page epigraph: 'I have a story to unfold ...' Every one of the novels contains its ruined buildings with their promised tales of tragedy and horror, no matter how early the date at which the action is set. The homology of architecture and physiognomy works both ways. Sometimes faces can assume the timeless hieroglyphic qualities of the ruin: the solemn and wild expression of St Aubert in *Udolpho*, which alerts his daughter to the existence of a family secret (*MU* 26); the extraordinary countenance of the monk Schedoni in *The Italian* which 'bore the traces of many passions, which seemed to have fixed the features they no longer animated' (*I.* 35). The wrecks of castles and human bodies alike testify to their function as theatres of the passions.

The curiosity aroused at the start of *A Sicilian Romance* is answered by a narrative designed more to tantalize than satisfy it. The original inhabitants of the castle are as mystified by their surroundings, as the present-day traveller is by the ruins. They see a light shining at night in the abandoned wing, and are unable to uncover its meaning until the penultimate chapter. The primordial crime is deeply buried. The clues that lead to it are vertiginous, one mystery giving way to another: the ultimate explanation always lies that much further in the past. Radcliffe's encryptment of criminal passion resembles that of Clara Reeve. As in Reeve, crime leaves its detritus like toxic waste to be discovered and disposed of by the next generation. But Radcliffe's management of the text, her employment of suspense and deferral, her scattering of clues and, above all, of false leads, is far more sophisticated (her critics would say, over-sophisticated). If the reader were to look back from the end-point of enlightenment over the preceding story, in the case of *The Old English Baron* she would see a straight path with perhaps a few short side-alleys, but in the case of any of Radcliffe's fictions, a vast concatenation of events seemingly unconnected at the time, but ultimately comprehensible as part of the grand plan of providence, or fate, or narrative desire.

The structure of past crime discovered and set to rights in the narrative present, which Radcliffe shares with Reeve, is the structure of tragicomedy. It contrasts with the tale of passion in present time, Sophia Lee's *The Recess*, the tragedies of Joanna Baillie, the novels of Charlotte Dacre. Where present passion invariably ends in disaster, retrospective passion can be mediated and redeemed. Happy endings are the preserve of tragicomedy. Reeve in *The Old English Baron* regulated access to originary evil and its dangerous effects through mimetic realism and moral sentiment, correctives to passion. Radcliffe's regulatory medium also includes moral sentiment, but, more important than the rhetoric of objective realism in her work, is the boldly subjective language of taste and imagination. It is a fact often overlooked that every one of her major heroines is said to possess creative genius. The admiring narrator shares with them an ardent appreciation of poetry, music, painting and the sublime and beautiful in nature, often giving rise to performance of their own compositions. It would be difficult to say where the artistic sensibility of the heroine ends and that of the narrator begins. Action, meaning itself, are sometimes almost lost in the swirling lyricism of Radcliffe's characteristic style. This quality was identified by an anonymous critic of the time with brilliant hyperbole: 'The sense floats in a poetical medium, and we are perplexed to account for the interest which it excites, till we recollect it may be compared to a corpse borne away on the tide, or the spectacle of a person struggling in the water.'[8]

In Radcliffe, the idea of destructive passions is countered by moral precept as one would expect; but also far more interestingly and seductively by representing the exaltation of creative passions. Strong feelings can safely be indulged, she suggests, because of their sublimation in aesthetic experience. This alchemical transformation is made possible by the tenet pronounced by St Aubert: 'Virtue and taste are nearly the same, for virtue is little more than active taste, and the most delicate affections of each combine in real love' (*MU* 49–50). The equation was well established in English aesthetic theory, from Shaftesbury through to Hazlitt. It was questioned by Jane Austen, no doubt with Radcliffe among others in mind, when she has the poetry-loving Marianne justify her unconventional conduct with her admirer Willoughby on the grounds of innate feeling, in *Sense and Sensibility*. Radcliffe herself implicitly complicates the rule when she gives certain villains a fine taste in music or art. That is why response to nature is the ultimate test for Radcliffe; only a sensibility uncorrupted by city life and social conventions is capable of it. There is also the risk of becoming vain of one's superior sensibility, warned against by St Aubert; there is an implied need for conversion into active good works, but the heroines seldom manage this beyond some well-intentioned sympathy. They are too much in need of charity themselves. Instead, for them, the pleasures of imagination are inward-turned, consolatory and fortifying. The narrator, the heroines, and sometimes the heroes, are drawn tightly together with the reader into a hedonistic community of taste which is virtuous by definition.

Behind Radcliffe's heroines stands the figure of the female artist as genius, transcendently actualized by Sarah Siddons. In the debut fiction *Athlin and Dunbayne*, Siddons lurks in the background. As Alison Milbank has observed, the plot of clan warfare and concealed identity is partly based on the popular Highland tragedy *Douglas* (1756) by John Home. The play provided Siddons with one of her best roles, as Matilda, Lady Randolph, and Radcliffe distributed the part between two characters: the widowed Countess Athlin and bereaved mother Baroness Malcolm. After this, Siddons's example was absorbed into the ingénue roles the actress was no longer prepared to play. But the traffic between Gothic fiction and the Kemble–Siddons theatrical dynasty intensified as Radcliffe reached the peak of her powers. In 1794, the year *Udolpho* was published, an operatic adaptation of *A Sicilian Romance* by Henry Siddons was successfully produced. *The Italian Monk*, an adaptation by Boaden, was acted at the Haymarket in August 1797, just seven months after the appearance of *The Italian*, with Vivaldi played by Charles Kemble, Sarah's brother. As far back as 1785 Sarah herself had acted the role of the wronged wife Hortensia in *The Count of Narbonne*, a stage version of *The Castle of Otranto*. In 1798 she played the considerably toned-down part of the she-devil in *Aurelio and Miranda*, a dramatization of *The Monk*.

But unlike Siddons, Radcliffe's Gothic heroines exemplify a variety of art for art's sake: their creativity is not vocational, with the partial exception of the working artist Ellena di Rosalba in *The Italian*. Their genius is bounded by the expectation of marriage and domestic bliss. Their immersion in poetry approximates the consolatory, recreational pleasures offered to the consumer of art, and most immediately, the Gothic reader.

THE EARLY WORKS

Already, in Radcliffe's first novel, the distinctions made between the inhabitants of the castles of Athlin and Dunbayne represent a first attempt to develop the contrast of creative and destructive passions. Osbert, Earl of Athlin, is a youth of 19: 'nature had given him a mind ardent and susceptible, to which education had added refinement and expansion. The visions of genius were bright in his imagination, and his heart, unchilled by the touch of disappointment, glowed with all the warmth of benevolence.' (*CAD* 4) The lord of neighbouring Dunbayne is the tyrant Baron Malcolm: 'torn by conflicting passions, he was himself the victim of their power' (*CAD* 39). The past crime which motivates the action is Osbert's underhand killing of the previous earl, leaving his widow, Matilda, and two children Osbert and Mary, desolate and vulnerable. Osbert resolves to avenge the murder and launches a surprise attack on Dunbayne, but he is captured and imprisoned. There he finds enigmatic signs of another instance of Malcolm's cruelty, in the discovery of two other prisoners, a mother and daughter. Meanwhile Malcolm presents an ultimatum that the beautiful Mary should be given to him in marriage, or Osbert will die. The terrible choice is complicated further by Mary's growing love for the valorous young peasant Alleyn, who engages in increasingly desperate attempts to free the earl. Finally Osbert escapes, Malcolm is killed in battle, and the female prisoners released. They have been revealed as the baron's sister-in-law, whose husband had been murdered and supplanted by his brother, and her daughter Laura. Alleyn (in accordance with sentimental convention) is found to be Baroness Malcolm's son Philip, believed dead. After a short digression – the abduction of Mary by a love-lorn Swiss count related to the baroness – Philip and Mary, and Osbert and Laura, are united with tidy symmetry.

Like Hamlet, or Edmund in *The Old English Baron*, Osbert seeks to revenge the death of his father. But like Hamlet again, he is not particularly successful as a man of action. His attempt to storm the castle of the villainous Baron Malcolm ends in capture and imprisonment. For much of the novel, he is a pawn in Malcolm's schemes: he faces execution if his sister Mary is not handed over as a bride to the murderer of their father. It is left to the peasant Alleyn to rescue Mary from various travails, free Osbert and bring about a happy denouement, in which it is discovered that he – Alleyn – is the true Baron Malcolm.

Yet, in spite of Osbert's largely passive role, he is nevertheless the gravitational centre of the narrative thanks to his imaginative 'genius'. Through him, the redemptive power of art is affirmed. For his characterization, Radcliffe draws on the well-established figure of the Celtic bard, who had featured in James Macpherson's hugely popular *Fingal* (1762), purportedly by the ancient Scottish poet Ossian, and James Beattie's *The Minstrel; or, the Progress of Genius* (1771–7), a tale of the evolution of artistic sensibility set in a Highland landscape, which also had an influence on William Wordsworth. The novel is set on the coast of north-east Scotland, 'the most romantic part of the Highlands' (*CAD* 3), in feudal times. These circumstances shape Osbert's imagination: 'wrapt in the bright visions of fancy', he 'would often lose himself in awful solitudes' (*CAD* 5). In imprisonment, when threatened by suicidal despair, he is sustained by the mysterious sound of a lute, and later a song delivered with 'impassioned tenderness' by a young lady imprisoned in the next dungeon. He reciprocates with a sonnet celebrating evening and fancy, written 'under the enthusiasm of the hour' (*CAD* 39). The restoration of virtue is marked by another composition by the earl, an ode on Morning, set to music by Mary.

Osbert's mediated self-expression through art is persistently contrasted with the unhindered eruption of feeling in Malcolm. Imagination – aesthetic sublimation of the passions – is both an index of virtue and a survival mechanism: it is the ability to reflect on and redirect feeling to desired ends. Against this is posited the tormented subjectivity of Malcolm, torn by conflicting impulses of pride, desire and sheer delight in cruelty. The character of Osbert, his misadventures and eventual triumph, are a rehearsal of the indestructible quality of genius which will henceforth be allotted to Radcliffe's heroines.

While the plot of *Athlin and Dunbayne* alludes to *The Old English Baron*, there is an obvious resemblance between *The Recess* and Radcliffe's next work, *A Sicilian Romance*, as if she were paying a conscious homage to her two most illustrious female forebears in the terror mode. As in the earlier novel, two sisters, Emilia and Julia, are raised in seclusion by a friend of their dead mother, Madame de Menon (like Mrs Marlow, she is the survivor of a tragic romance). Their existence is a sort of paradise of high culture: 'Books, music, and painting, divided the hours of her leisure, and many beautiful summer-evenings were spent in the pavilion, where the refined conversation of madame, the poetry of Tasso, the lute of Julia, and the friendship of Emilia, combined to form a species of happiness, such as elevated and highly susceptible minds are alone capable of receiving or communicating' (*SR* 7). But the paradise is also a prison: they are kept there by order of their father Ferdinand, Marquis of Mazzini, 'a man of a voluptuous and imperious character', or rather, of his second wife, Maria de Vollorno, herself 'of unconquerable spirit' and able to bend her husband's passions to her will (*SR* 3). Julia, like Lee's heroines, has an ardent temperament: her 'eyes were dark, and full of fire, but tempered with modest sweetness'. Like them, she yearns to experience the wider world.

The plot begins with the return of the marquis and his wife to the castle of Mazzini to celebrate the majority of his only son Ferdinand, who had been raised with him in Naples. Ferdinand is accompanied by his friend Hippolitus, Count Vereza, loved unrequitedly by the dissolute marchesa, and at first sight by Julia. Julia discovers her love is returned but soon learns also that she is intended by the marquis for the Duke de Luovo, a double of Julia's father, in whom the love of power is the governing passion. From this point Julia's existence becomes an alternation of imprisonment and flight. An elopement planned by Ferdinand and Hippolitus fails and, believing her lover dead, Julia manages to escape the castle with the help of servants. She seeks asylum in an abbey, where the *Abate* soon proves as tyrannical as her pursuers. Her adventures include a shipwreck and capture by banditti. Eventually she stumbles by chance upon the hidden entrance to an apartment of her father's castle, within which she discovers her mother, still alive, having been shut up there by the marquis when he wished to take another wife. Julia remains with her in concealment, while the villainous couple destroy each other. Maria is found with a lover by the marquis and takes revenge on his jealousy by poisoning him and herself. Ferdinand and Hippolitus, both of whom had been believed dead, reappear, and all ends happily.

Two important features of Radcliffe's art were introduced in this novel: fear of the supernatural and, as already mentioned, the transfer of creative genius from the hero to the central female character. Supernaturalism is barely employed in *Athlin and Dunbayne*. There are three points at which one character briefly mistakes another for a ghost, and this was as far as Lee had gone in *The Recess*. But with *A Sicilian Romance*, Radcliffe made such a misapprehension a major strand in the narrative, running from the beginning almost until the end. A light is seen moving through the deserted wing of the castle, and groans are heard. Julia and Emilia, along with the servants, instantly conclude there is a ghost, and even Madame de Menon admits that 'such beings *may* exist' (*SR* 36). Ferdinand goes searching through the ruined chambers, but finds nothing. Only the marquis takes a trenchantly rationalist stance and ridicules their superstition – as well he might, being the only one who knows that the source of these effects is his imprisoned first wife, Louisa. But the mystery is only revealed in the final section, giving plenty of opportunity in the meantime for the reader's nerves to be pleasurably frayed.

I have outlined in the Introduction how the taste for superstition was being recuperated in the course of the century, as one of the attributes of original genius (see p. 8–9). William Duff in his *Essay on Original Genius*, published in 1767, conceived the preternatural to be the final frontier of aesthetic endeavour, into which only the most daring souls will venture. Shakespeare, he declares, 'is the only *English* writer, who with amazing boldness has ventured to burst the barriers of a separate state, and disclose the land of Apparitions, Shadows, and Dreams; and he has nobly succeeded in his daring attempt', adding that 'none but a Genius uncommonly original, can hope for success in the pursuit'.[9] Belief was irrelevant to this new kind of ghost-seeing. The ability to evoke supernatural dread was presented by Duff and other writers as the ultimate test of a truly unbounded imagination.

Radcliffe took up the challenge, though in a rather ambivalent way. In her fictions, the servants alone give whole-hearted credit to the signs of a haunting. The educated characters all waver between scepticism and the apparent evidence of their senses.

The narrator plays a duplicitous role, now luring the reader into blood-curdling apprehensions by 'objective' description or the recounting of rumours, now sententiously excusing the heroine for a temporary lapse into irrationalism. And in the end, apparently supernatural phenomena are always explained by natural causes. Radcliffe employed the device of the 'explained supernatural' in all the novels published in her lifetime. It became her trademark, and was also widely imitated. The explanation is relatively straightforward in *A Sicilian Romance*, but as her novels became longer and the plots more complex, so instances of supernaturalism multiplied, and the means of explaining them naturalistically rather more tortuous. Some critics complained that foreknowledge of the device spoiled the effect of her later works.

Why did Radcliffe not stick to her guns and include 'real' ghosts? It is a question even her first biographer, Thomas Talfourd, asked, and failed to answer to his own satisfaction. Some see it as pusillanimity, a failure of artistic nerve; others as a matter of social propriety, more pressing on a female author. In fact, in her last novel *Gaston de Blondeville* she did include the supernatural unexplained, but the work was a sort of throwback to the cautious descriptiveness of Reeve and has none of the magic of her famous works. We are returned, then, to the tension between plot – those aspects of narrative pleasure exhausted by one reading (or less, if the method becomes predictable) – and poetry, the display of imaginative power. It is almost as if Radcliffe gloried in the contradiction, exaggerating it as she gains confidence as an author: she milks the supernatural situations for all they're worth, supporting them with a panoply of ominous epigraphs from Shakespeare or Collins, and then in the end tosses them away like worthless husks.

Late in life William Duff, the expert on genius, published *Letters on the Intellectual and Moral Character of Women* (1807), in which he claimed that the 'delicate organization of [the female] frame' was 'obstructive of, if not incompatible with' the 'highest species of invention ... to the attainment of which a creative energy and masculine vigour of mind, are indispensably requisite'. As an example of 'exalted genius' he specifically marks out 'the talent of inventing and exhibiting supernatural characters, with their proper insignia and attributes'.[10] To be fair, it must be admitted that he identifies only three authors in the past 'six thousand years' – Homer, Shakespeare and Milton – as having achieved this height. But this qualification did not protect him from being challenged by a reviewer, who cited the example of Radcliffe to refute the point.[11] The exchange suggests that the fact that the supernatural is 'explained away' was less important than some, notably Walter Scott, would allow. Radcliffe was a ghost-seer in imagination: the objective 'reality' of the phantasmal is less important than the strength of its subjective effect. The reviewer's rebuke also suggests that, like Siddons, Radcliffe had succeeded in shaking the assumption that original genius was the monopoly of men.

Julia, the heroine of *A Sicilian Romance*, we are told at the first opportunity, has an 'ardent imagination' and 'her mind early exhibited the symptoms of genius' (*SR* 4). Her sister Emilia is a talented draughtswoman, but her story is soon pushed to the margins of the narrative. Julia is a musician, and Radcliffe consistently elevates the non-mimetic arts of music and lyric poetry over drawing.

> The instructions of madame she caught with astonishing quickness, and in a short time attained to a degree of excellence in her favorite study, which *few persons have ever exceeded. Her manner was entirely her own.* It was not in the rapid intricacies of execution, that she excelled so much as in that delicacy of taste, and in those enchanting powers of expression, which seem to breathe a soul through the sound, and which take captive the heart of the hearer. (*SR* 4–5; emphasis added)

This enthusiastic passage is of great significance in Radcliffe's work. It marks the creation of the persona of the heroine as artist and as author-surrogate; a figure which, like the explained supernatural, became a trademark. The introduction of this type relates closely to her own self-identity and public recognition as a female author. Reviewers of the first novel had assumed that the author was male. Although *Sicilian Romance* was also anonymous, it was generally assumed to be female-authored. After the notable success of *The Romance of the Forest*, she put her name, 'Ann Radcliffe' (*not* 'Mrs Radcliffe'), to the second edition, and every following publication.

The heroine-as-original-genius provides a new principle of coherence for Radcliffe's narrative. In Julia, the scattered elements of *Athlin and Dunbayne* are brought together. She has the sensitivity to landscape and poetic inspiration of Osbert, the talents on the lute of Laura and Mary. She provides the accompaniment for her own compositions, and this unification of the arts is also a symbolic binding of plot and poetry. The narration is organized around her ever-active sensibility, capable of soaring above all difficulties, while the action centres on the endangerment of her vulnerable female body. This is the model used in the next two novels.

The Romance of the Forest begins uncharacteristically, and dramatically, *in medias res*. The identity of the heroine, Adeline, is initially unknown. She is first glimpsed as an object of pity, threatened by ruffians, taken in out of charity by Monsieur La Motte and his wife, who are themselves fleeing from imprisonment for debt in Paris. But as they journey towards the south, Adeline's capacity for sublime feeling quickly becomes apparent (*RF* 14, 22), and her superiority is soon confirmed by the narrator: 'The observations and general behaviour of Adeline already bespoke a good understanding and an amiable heart, but she had yet more – she had genius' (*RF* 29).

Once installed with the La Mottes in the relative peace of a ruined abbey in Fontangville [sic] Forest, Adeline is able to give vent to her inspiration in a series of improvised poems: 'To the Visions of Fancy' (*RF* 35), a pastiche of Joseph Warton which celebrates the elevation of sentiment to 'passion true'; a meditation on the pleasures of terror and melancholy, 'Night' (*RF* 83), and another paean to melancholy, 'Sonnet To the Lilly', an exercise in autobiography and poetic transference, of which the unknown Theodore (her future husband) is an enraptured auditor. Uniquely, Radcliffe headed this novel with a note acknowledging the previous publication of the poems: the editor Chloe Chard remarks that 'Song of a Spirit' was printed in the *Gazeteer and New Daily Advertiser*, under the name 'Adeline' – an unmistakable instance of the identification of the author with her genius heroine.[12]

But there are many threats to Adeline's peace, both inside and outside the abbey. Madame La Motte becomes jealous of her and treats her harshly. There are strange stories about the abbey itself, repeated by the servant Peter: Adeline has a series of dreams, and discovers a manuscript, which indicate that a murder was committed there. They all live in constant fear of discovery, the La Mottes by the law, and Adeline by her father, who had tried to force her to take the veil and then abandoned her to the villains from whom she was rescued at the outset of the story. Before long their solitude is broken by the Marquis de Montalt, who seems at first a model of cultivated politeness, but soon reveals designs to seduce Adeline and blackmail La Motte. Adeline must be saved from his clutches twice, once with the help of Theodore, the marquis's adjutant, who pays for his gallantry with imprisonment for desertion, and a second time by La Motte, who recoils from murdering her, once the marquis's lust turns mysteriously homicidal. With the faithful Peter, Adeline flees from France to Savoy, where she finds refuge with the benevolent minister La Luc and his family. It is discovered that Theodore is La Luc's son and that Adeline is the niece of the marquis, her father having been murdered by him from greed (the man she believed to be her father was the henchman of her uncle). Theodore and La Motte are released from prison by the clemency of the authorities, and the marquis dies by poisoning himself while awaiting trial. Adeline inherits the marquis's property, and marries Theodore.

As usual, a bare recounting of the plot does little to suggest what is significant about Radcliffe's fiction. *The Romance of the Forest* is, among other things, a fascinating novel of ideas. Adeline's dependence on the kindness of strangers raises issues about ethics and human nature, with direct allusion to Rousseau, and uncanny parallels with de Sade's contemporary novel *Justine, or The Misfortunes of Virtue*.[13] Here, more than elsewhere in her writing, Radcliffe questions the equation of taste and virtue. The château of the marquis, where Adeline is imprisoned while he attempts to corrupt her, is a temple of aesthetic pleasure. Art is put to the service of illicit passions, yet it retains the power to charm. Later in the novel, Radcliffe seems still to be wrestling with the problem, in a lengthy parable of La Luc's daughter Clara and her selfish passion for lute-playing, conquered in the end by the higher pleasure of philanthropy.

But there is no ambivalence in the portrayal of Adeline, who is both good and brilliant. Radcliffe channels all her aesthetic idealism through her heroine. She is susceptible to the music ordered by the marquis, but it elevates her mind to a degree which intimidates him and enables her escape. Taste makes her the equal of any man. Her romance with Theodore is mediated by art. He is first attracted by overhearing one of her private recitals; he displays, like her, 'many of the qualities of genius' and shows a 'similarity of taste and opinion': 'Their discourse was enriched by elegant literature, and endeared by mutual regard' (RF 190). In Savoy, Adeline speaks the same language with Theodore's father, the flawless M. La Luc. She engages with him in 'rational conversation', and roams freely in his library, where (in a standard Radcliffe touch) she picks out the works of Shakespeare and Milton, having fortunately studied English during her convent education, and learnt to distinguish the superiorities of the English over the French in poetry (RF 260–61; Milton had not completed Paradise Lost at the time the novel is set, in 1658). She also wanders the countryside alone, rapturously viewing the mountain scenery and composing stanzas in tribute to it.

She is saved from priggishness, however, by the extremity of her circumstances, and by the energy of the responses Radcliffe attributes to her. She follows the type of the Gothic heroine who actively rebels against confinement, and claims her right to life, liberty, and the free play of imagination, in spite of the dangers of the world at large (The Romance of the Forest was written at a time when British opinion on the French Revolution was still in its honeymoon period; including that of William Radcliffe's newspaper the English Chronicle). Adeline is courageous (RF 62, 113), her sympathy for others is based on healthy self-love rather than selflessness (RF 82), she is willing to break with propriety in the interests of self-preservation (e.g. RF 103, 106–7, 164). Even her frequent habit of fainting proves to be a valuable survival skill (e.g. RF 158, 176). And when the situation demands, she is perfectly capable of running (RF 166–7).

The adventures of her imagination are equally remarkable. The bare bones of Peter's account of the abbey take on life in her dreams, perhaps the most powerful, strange, and enduringly frightening examples of Radcliffe's supernaturalist writing, since in this case she was under no compulsion to explain them away (RF 41, 108–10). The following night, her exploration of a series of hidden chambers is experienced as an extension of her dream-world. She discovers a room identical to that in which she had visualized a dying man, and is nearly overcome by superstitious dread. Searching further she finds a dagger and a roll of manuscript. The handwritten journal describes the mental torments of an unnamed prisoner, a Gothic novel in miniature, and turns Adeline into an avid and suggestible reader, a model consumer of Gothic. She weeps and startles, imagining that she hears the words on the page being whispered behind her, and sees a figure moving in the shadows of the room. The exercise of her feelings is soon applied on her own behalf, when almost at once she finds herself in the power of the marquis. Her attempts at escape are surreal episodes of mistaken identity and unnavigable space. She manages to jump from the window of the château only to lose herself in the menacing calm of a moonlit landscape garden in the English style (again, a blithe anachronism). She approaches a light to seek help, then sees through the window, as in a nightmare, the marquis stretched out drunk in a pavilion. She runs back aimlessly into the night. 'To her imagination the grounds were boundless; she had wandered from lawn to lawn, and from grove to grove, without perceiving any termination to the place' (*RF* 166). 'Capability' Brown had a lot to answer for. Finally Theodore appears from nowhere with a carriage to whisk her away. But it is not long before he, by a kind of contagion, is also a prisoner in the marquis's hands, having been wounded in a duel by an officer come to reclaim Adeline. Later, once she is removed to Savoy and safety, she continues to dream, awake and asleep, of a prisoner, this time Theodore, wounded and despairing (*RF* 217, 229). The chief fascination of the narrative consists in this perpetual overlapping of dream and reality, punctuated by poems and epigraphs which celebrate formally the process of imaginative transfiguration.

It is not surprising that novels focusing on female genius should have been eagerly read and enthusiastically approved by female writers of the day. The bluestockings who had featured in the social scene of Radcliffe's youth in Bath were quick to appreciate her work. Elizabeth Carter wrote to her friend Mrs Montagu early in 1790, praising *A Sicilian Romance* and speculating on the identity of the author.[14] Later a friend reported that she 'expresses herself in a very strong manner in favour of the "*Mysteries of Udolpho*" and of the talents of Mrs

72

Radcliffe, the author'. Anna Seward's interest must have been piqued by finding herself included among the quoted authors in *The Romance of the Forest*; she admired Radcliffe's scene-paintings, though finding them overlong.[15] Hester Lynch Piozzi would have been struck by silent borrowings from her travelogue *Observations and Reflections Made in the Course of a Journey through France, Italy and Germany* (1789) in *Udolpho* and *The Italian*. Perhaps this accounts for her dry riposte to one who ventured to compare *Udolpho* with *Macbeth* for horror, 'Yes truly replied H:L:P. as like as Pepper-Mint Water is to good Brandy'.[16] Nevertheless she remarked in the same breath that Radcliffe's 'tricks used to frighten Mrs Siddons [a close friend] and me very much', and was happy to report another comment which humorously associated her with Radcliffe's poeticizing heroines: 'Cecilia says that like Emily the moment my Mind or my Teeth are at Ease for an Instant, I set about *arranging* a few Stanzas'.[17]

THE LATER WORKS

The Mysteries of Udolpho is not only the best-known Gothic novel of the 1790s, but one of the most extraordinary works of English literature produced in the eighteenth century. This is not to say that its four substantial volumes are free of absurdities or longueurs. It is not always an easy read, but that is of a piece with the scale of its ambitions. The novel has been casually belittled by many twentieth-century critics, most of whom seem not have looked beyond the scenes featuring the villain Montoni and have therefore missed much of its importance. Feminist criticism has brought about the recuperation of the author, and *Udolpho* is now available in an edition that does it justice, with an introduction and notes by Terry Castle, one of its best interpreters.

My claims for *Udolpho* will appear far-fetched to some. I am willing to admit that Radcliffe's style is at times repetitive and formulaic. She is not the most witty or intellectually agile of writers, though the narration is not without irony, and the ideological debates conducted by her characters are more incisive and topical than has often been credited. There are some botched aspects to the plot, which will be discussed. But the plot nevertheless serves its purpose, which is to lure readers into a world of heightened aesthetic experience and keep them there. Radcliffe's aim was to produce a total work of art: she attempted to invest the novel form, still in its first experimental stage, with the qualities of poetry, music and painting. Can anything similar be found in Defoe, Richardson, Fielding, Burney or Austen? Radcliffe was a great original, a fact recognized at the time and for some time afterwards, though rivals like Walter Scott were inclined to pay her backhanded compliments which eroded her reputation, until eventually her works were unread and unregarded. Even Scott, however, could pay a handsome tribute:

> Indeed, the praise may be claimed for Mrs Radcliffe, of having been the first to introduce into her prose fictions a beautiful and fanciful tone of natural description and impressive narrative, which had hitherto been exclusively applied to poetry... [She] has a title to be considered as the first poetess of romantic fiction, that is, if actual rhythm shall not be deemed essential to poetry.[18]

The reader of *Udolpho* is given fair warning of the innovative nature of the experience in store for them. No Gothic fiction before or since can have risked such a slow and diffuse opening section. With only a few shimmering fragments of mystery to go on – a glimpse of St Aubert kissing the portrait of an unknown woman, his dying instruction to Emily to burn his papers without looking at them – the reader is led on an apparent wild-goose chase from La Vallée, the idyllic home of the St Aubert family, across the Pyrénées with the valetudinarian Monsieur St Aubert, his daughter Emily, and Valancourt, a young gentleman on a walking tour who joins their party. St Aubert dies in Languedoc, and the grieving Emily returns to La Vallée to await the instructions of her aunt Madame Cheron, now her guardian.

Travel operates as a self-reflexive metaphor for the narrative journey itself in these early episodes. The first chapter is interrupted by a slyly pertinent ode to the glow-worm who, under orders from the fairies, leads the benighted traveller astray and leaves him in the mire. The occasion of the ode is an extended conversation between Emily and her father, on the pleasures of fancy. There will be many such interruptions, and many such digressions on fancy and imagination. The tour through the Pyrénées, which extends through five chapters, is a perfect allegory for the conduct of the narrative, and at the same time a training-course. The elevation of mountains and elevation of souls mirror each other, and the reader quickly learns that elevation means circumlocution. While the mule-drawn coach labours along the stony path and up steep ascents, the travellers wander off on foot at every opportunity to admire the view from a cliff-top or enjoy the shade of nearby groves. So caught up are they in the visions of sublimity that day after day they forget the time and find themselves lost in the dark, in danger from roving banditti (who, however, never actually appear). In this manner the reader is (ideally) broken in to the delays found at every stage of the story, and taught to abandon herself to the delights of static reverie. The best result would be a revaluation of narrative pleasure, demoting the instant gratifications of plot in favour of a more patient and sensuous interaction with the text.

But at the same time it would be a mistake to exaggerate an opposition or hierarchy of aesthetic sense and plot in *Udolpho*. To some extent they cohere. The plot is driven by suspicion and curiosity, faculties linked to the workings of imagination. And the plot is at times foregrounded, notably in the middle section of the novel set in the fortress of Udolpho. Before Emily arrives at this destination, there are other journeys. She goes to Toulouse to live with her aunt, who gives her permission to marry Valancourt only to withdraw it when she herself marries the haughty Italian, Signor Montoni. They journey to Italy, taking in Venice on the way to Montoni's remote castle in the Apennines. There Emily's terrors really begin. She is pressured to marry one of Montoni's unsavoury associates, while her aunt fades and dies under her husband's ill-treatment. Meanwhile rumours circulate that Montoni was responsible for the murder of Laurentini di Udolpho, his lover and the previous owner of Udolpho, and Emily is unable to resist the idea that the castle is haunted. Along with Du Pont, a fellow prisoner, her maid Annette and Ludovico, Annette's fiancé, she escapes.

The ship that carries them to France is wrecked off the coast of Languedoc, and the fugitives are given hospitality at the Chateau-le-Blanc, home of the De Villefort family, close to where St Aubert died. Here, further mysteries unfold. It appears that in this place too the previous lady of the house was murdered, and the housekeeper Dorothée notes Emily's striking resemblance to her. Ludovico offers to keep watch in the allegedly haunted chambers, and vanishes. The 'ghost' is explained when Count De Villefort and his daughter Blanche are captured by banditti, rediscover Ludovico, and find that the abandoned rooms have been used to store stolen goods. The mad Sister Agnes at a nearby convent turns out to be Laurentini, who confesses to having left Udolpho to pursue her passion for the late Marquis de Villeroi, and to poisoning the count's wife. The ill-fated countess was St Aubert's sister; her death was his terrible secret. There is one final problem to resolve: Valancourt resurfaces at Chateau-le-Blanc having passed the time of Emily's absence living the high life in Paris, and trailing a reputation as a card sharp and kept man. He must be cleared of the worst allegations before they are reunited. Emily inherits the property of Laurentini and Madame Cheron-Montoni, but returns to La Vallée to lead an existence of rural retirement.

The primordial passion in this history, the evil from which all others stem, turns out to be Laurentini's illicit love for the count and its murderous outcome: 'a crime, which whole years of repentance and of the severest penance had not been able to obliterate from her conscience' (*MU* 664). The suspicions directed against Montoni, and the affective power of his characterization, were therefore an ingenious blind. This sleight-of-hand, though it keeps the reader guessing to the end, also unavoidably leaves a sense of having been duped. Once Emily leaves Udolpho, the previously all-powerful, charismatic Montoni disappears from view: 'he had become a clod of earth, and his life was vanished like a shadow!' (*MU* 580). We are given a final brief report that he has died of poison, probably self-administered, after falling into the hands of the Inquisition in Venice. He is forgotten, while Laurentini's history takes centre-stage. The character of Montoni is in this way the equivalent of Radcliffe's most notorious device for the creation of suspense, the Black Veil. The veil we are told conceals a picture at Udolpho which has 'something very dreadful about it' and some connection with the previous owner of the castle (*MU* 233). Emily's curiosity is aroused; she goes to the chamber on her own, lifts the veil, and promptly faints (see Fig. 4). When

Fig. 4. An illustration from a French edition of Ann Radcliffe's
The Mysteries of Udolpho (Paris, 1798).

she recovers she resolves not to reveal her knowledge of the secret, and the narrator keeps equally silent. It is only in a clumsy aside in the final pages that the narrator reveals what was behind the veil: a wax effigy of a decaying body designed as an object of meditation for some penitent, which Emily imagined to be Montoni's victim.

It is easy enough to outline the plot and criticize its mechanisms. But they are only one part of the reader's affective engagement with the novel. Affect is not dependent on probability, nor is it exhausted by the quest for elucidation. As I tried to show with reference to *The Romance of the Forest*, Radcliffe's skill lies in blurring the boundary between objective description and imaginary illusion. Her interest is in altered states of mind, for better or for worse. Frequently in that novel the narrator speaks of reading as a surrender to illusion, and books as opiates (e.g. *RF* 35, 82, 208). Walter Scott, taking the cue, compares the reading of Radcliffe's own work to 'the use of opiates, baneful when habitually and constantly resorted to, but of most blessed power in those moments of pain and of languor, when the whole head is sore and the whole heart sick'.[19] Emily, like all her heroines, is a creature of extremes. Her imagination, feeding off art or nature, can make the world a paradise or a hell. Incarcerated at Udolpho, 'Her present life appeared like the dream of a distempered imagination, or like one of those frightful fictions, in which the wild genius of the poets sometimes delighted' (*MU* 296).

More often, imagination is a resource for the heroine, allowing her to moderate passions into sentiment, or translate emotion from worldly objects to ideas of the divine. The action halts while Emily endeavours to 'amuse her fancy' by envisioning the view from her window as a picturesque landscape painting; (*MU* 240; cf. *MU* 244–5). When even poetry-reading and sketching fail to ward off feelings of dread, music retains its powers. Music holds a high status in Radcliffe's assessment of affect. In all her works she comments on its ability to arouse, elevate, or soothe emotions. As a non-mimetic form of expression, it was thought to work more immediately on the mind. In this novel, music exemplifies the relative autonomy of aesthetic affect from plot: it is dextrously interwoven with the unfolding narrative, yet also tangential to the central action.

Throughout, Emily periodically falls under the spell of melodies with no apparent source. In the grounds of La Vallée, at the start, Emily is transfixed by the sound of an exquisite air, played on her own lute (*MU* 9). In Languedoc, near Chateau-le-Blanc, a guitar accompanied by a sweet voice is often heard at night, leading to the belief that the woods are haunted, and that the sound is an omen of death (*MU* 68). Later, during the worst moments at Udolpho, when Emily expects every day to hear of the murder of her aunt, she is visited at night by 'delicious sounds' that at once arouse her superstition and a fortifying religious awe (*MU* 330; cf. *MU* 340, 355, 386–7, 416, 439, 443, 446). The explanations given for these performances are frankly bathetic: at La Vallée and Udolpho, the musician is Monsieur Du Pont, a neighbour who loves Emily, is coincidentally captured by Montoni's men while on military service in Italy, and discreetly vanishes with the return of Valancourt; in Languedoc, it is Sister Agnes, who wanders the woods in the manner normal to plaintive madwomen. As so often in *Udolpho*, Radcliffe obviously considered that a measure of absurdity was a fair price to pay for long passages of beauty and power.

The Italian; or The Confessional of the Black Penitents contains the single most celebrated instance of Radcliffe's use of music. The occasion is a meeting between the Marchesa di Vivaldi whose ruling passion of pride is outraged by her son's determination to marry Ellena Rosalba, a woman without rank or fortune, and Father Schedoni, her confessor, who fears that the young Vivaldi knows something of his shadowy past, and seeks revenge on him. The scene is the church of San Nicolo, in a deserted cloister at dusk. He endeavours by sophistry to persuade her that the murder of Ellena is morally justified, and she is on the point of concurring, when the strains of a requiem reanimate conscience and compassion in her. While she retires to weep, he rages inwardly:

> 'Behold, what is woman!' said he – 'The slave of her passions, the dupe of her senses! When pride and revenge speak in her breast; she defies obstacles, and laughs at crimes! Assail but her senses, let music, for instance, touch some feeble chord of her heart, and echo to her fancy, and lo! all her perceptions change: – she shrinks from the act she had but an instant before believed meritorious, yields to some new emotion, and sinks – the victim of a sound! O, weak and

contemptible being!' (*I.* 178)

The narrator comments, with a theoretical precision in the treatment of interiority which is new to Radcliffe, 'The desperate passions, which had resisted every remonstrance of reason and humanity, were vanquished only by other passions' (*I.* 178). The striking synthesis of narrative drama and aesthetic affect in this episode is part of a change of direction, and a new assurance in her practice as a story-teller.

It seems likely that, in *The Italian*, Radcliffe responded to certain criticisms of *Udolpho*: she interspersed no poetry in this story, cut down on landscape description (though it is still plentiful), and considerably shortened the overall length (three volumes to *Udolpho's* four). But there was another, more positive, reason to make changes. Radcliffe now had nothing to prove. *Udolpho* had been almost universally hailed as a brilliant achievement. It was around this time that rumours of her spectacular earnings began to circulate, as they would continue to do well into the nineteenth century. Scott reported that for *Udolpho* 'the booksellers felt themselves authorized in offering what was then considered as an unprecedented sum, £500'.[20] In 1821 an article on authors' profits in the *Gentleman's Magazine* upped the rumoured sum to £1,000. For *The Italian* she received £800. As Charles Lamb wrote in a letter to William Godwin, 'such things *sell*'.[21]

It is telling that at this stage Radcliffe chose to abandon her *alter ego*, the heroine-poet, having thoroughly established her own creative genius. Ellena is not a poet, though she is endowed with impeccable taste. She is an adept at needlework who 'passed whole days in embroidering silks', and a copyist who produces drawings based on the antique. Moreover, she works for money, to support herself and her aunt Signora Bianchi. In the interests of increased complexity and suspense, she shares the limelight with the hero, the narrative moving between their separate adventures. This is a drastic shift in the heroine's status, and with it Radcliffe seems to announce a new and more businesslike attitude to narration.

A related shift is the more immediate and explicit representation of the passions. As before, the narrative is organized around the apprehension and gradual revelation of past crime. But whereas in the previous novels the traces of crime in the present day are delicately suggested, in *The Italian* they are evoked with ferocious energy in the second chapter, when Schedoni is introduced:

> His figure was striking, but not so from grace; it was tall, and, though extremely thin, his limbs were large and uncouth, and as he stalked along, wrapt in the black garments of his order, there was something terrible in its air; something almost super-human. His cowl, too, as it threw a shade over the livid paleness of his face, encreased its severe character, and gave an effect to his large melancholy eye, which approached to horror. His was not the melancholy of a sensible and wounded heart, but apparently that of a gloomy and ferocious disposition. There was something in his physiognomy extremely singular, and that can not easily be defined. It bore the traces of many passions, which seemed to have fixed the features they no longer animated. An habitual gloom and severity prevailed over the deep lines of his countenance; and his eyes were so piercing that they seemed to penetrate, at a single glance, into the hearts of men, and to read their most secret thoughts; few persons could support their scrutiny, or even endure to meet them twice. Yet, notwith-standing all this gloom and austerity, some rare occasions of interest had called forth a character upon his countenance entirely different; and he could adapt himself to the tempers and passions of persons, he wished to conciliate, with astonishing facility, and generally with complete triumph. (*I*. 34–5)

It would be impossible for the reader not to feel, like Vivaldi, 'a shuddering presentiment of what this monk was preparing for him' (*I*. 35). Only the nature of the confession remains to be told. But I quote the portrait of Schedoni at length because it also seems to embody a new authorial ideal. The intrepid investigation of his 'depths' is accompanied by an emphasis on his own powers of penetration: his skill at eliciting and reading the passions of others. By possessing this ability, the complex villain becomes the counterpart of the author, displacing the heroine from her reflexive function, just as she is displaced by him as the affective centre of the narrative.

At the same time, the new prominence of the villain entails a temporal change in the treatment of the passions. The darkest criminality is no longer restricted to the past tense and mediated by the passage of time, with only its reverberations felt in the present. It is now witnessed at close quarters, active and immediate, in the plot to murder Ellena. The assassination

81

scene is a long time in preparation. Schedoni's introduction of the idea, and the marchesa's wavering acquiescence have already been mentioned. This layer of suspense gives way to a second, when Ellena is taken by force to an isolated house on the shores of the Adriatic. She endures a period of dreadful uncertainty in the keeping of Spalatro, a double of Schedoni: 'She had never before seen villainy and suffering so strongly pictured on the same face, and she observed him with a degree of thrilling curiosity, which for a moment excluded from her mind all consciousness of the evils to be apprehended from him' (*I*. 210). But fear is not suspended for long: she watches terrified in the dark; she suspects the food he gives her is poisoned. When she is inexplicably given permission to walk on the beach, a brief hope of gaining freedom is dashed by the sudden and dramatic entrance of Schedoni himself. Here the focus moves from Ellena's distress to the monk's agitated countenance and contradictory impulses, hesitating between vengeful fury and pity. The narration next begins to delve into his past (while withholding sufficient information for a final denouement) in order to further animate his inner struggle. From this point in the episode, Ellena's role is entirely passive, she sleeps while Schedoni and Spalatro delay and quarrel over who must murder the girl. Finally Schedoni lifts the dagger (in a gesture which carries resonances of sexual assault), but is halted by the sight of a miniature of himself hanging round her neck, which reveals him to be her father. The resulting volte-face provides further glimpses into the workings of the monk's tormented soul.

The eclipse of the heroine in favour of the villain is partial rather than absolute. Her trials, as indicated, are vivid enough, and in the earlier part of the novel her sensibility and strength of mind are given full play. When she is first abducted and imprisoned at the convent at San Stefano, she successfully resists pressure to submit to an arranged marriage or take the veil. Vivaldi and his servant Paolo rescue her, but they soon fall into Schedoni's clutches again. Vivaldi is arrested for abducting a nun on the orders of the Inquisition. Ellena is subjected to the ordeal already described, and acquires a 'father'. Schedoni now wishes to promote the marriage with Vivaldi, but the latter is immured in the prison of the Inquisition in Rome, threatened with a slow death by torture.

Vivaldi is visited in his cell, however, by a mysterious, possibly supernatural, cowled being, who tells him how to incriminate Schedoni. The attention of the tribunal is redirected to the monk, and he is eventually discovered to be the nobleman Count di Bruno, who secretly murdered his brother in order to possess his wife. He forces her to marry him, and then murders her as well when she is suspected of adultery, before taking refuge in the order of the Black Penitents. Schedoni himself only confesses his crimes in his dying moments, having administered poison to his accuser and former associate the monk Nicola di Zampari, and taken it himself. The marchesa dies repentent. It has emerged that Ellena is in fact the daughter of the murdered brother, and that Sister Olivia, a nun who had aided her at San Stefano, is her mother, not dead after all. Vivaldi and Ellena are wed.

The primordial crime revealed at the end would be familiar enough to the reader of Gothic. Displaced in any case by the emphasis on present-time villainy, it is a quaint reprise of the mainspring of *The Old English Baron* and *The Romance of the Forest*: the jealousy of the younger brother, a mixture of sexual motive and rebellion against primogeniture. These motives are over-shadowed in the action by the marchesa's passion of class pride. This was the first time Radcliffe had dealt with the issue since *Athlin and Dunbayne*; her stance is liberal, within limits. The narration condemns class prejudice in the characters, but the plot nevertheless prepares to elevate the lower-class protagonist to an acceptable rank. At the same time, however, servants assume an increasing prominence in Radcliffe's novels. In *Romance of the Forest*, Peter is instrumental in the plot and serves occasionally to lighten the tension, but he is still marginal. In *Udolpho* the servant couple Annette and Ludovico play a significant role, as do to a lesser extent Theresa and Dorothée, the housekeepers at La Vallée and Chateau-le-Blanc. But Paolo in *The Italian* is from the start Vivaldi's loyal companion; they form almost a comic partnership. He contributes to the broadened spectrum of feeling in the novel, providing consistent light relief to counterbalance the intensified darkness of Schedoni. It is possible that Radcliffe now had more determined aspirations to achieve the range of laughter and terror found in Shakespeare's tragedies, which Walpole, too, had attempted in *Otranto*.

Radcliffe stopped publishing at the height of her powers. She remained a potent influence on the next generation of Gothic writers. Her memory was kept alive, not only by new editions of her work and adaptations for the stage, but also by frequent retrospective articles in the periodicals. Probably the most resonant judgement among the many eulogies was that put forward in an 'Estimate of the Literary Character of Mrs Ann Ratcliffe [sic]' in the *Monthly Magazine* in 1819.[22] Its general concern is with the distinction between mediocrity and excellence, and specifically with the inability of Radcliffe's many imitators to recapture 'the magic of her imagination'. Going on to a more detailed account of her gifts, the writer compares the murder scene in *Macbeth* with the attempted assassination of Ellena in *The Italian* and prefers the latter for its greater simplicity and the 'aërial haze of poetical penciling' no less fine than that of Shakespeare. It is argued that Radcliffe is a true original, derivative neither of Walpole (who is too laughably extreme) nor the German horror-novelists (who exaggerate the passions). Her villains Montoni and Schedoni are placed in the company of Schiller's Karl Moor and Byron's Corsair and Lara: she has 'dissected depravity with *medean* boldness, and dared to lay open the arteries of *male* dereliction from the oracles of the heart to the marrow in the bones. She has penetrated beyond the metaphysics of her sex, and exposed the criminality peculiar to ours'. Her enchantment is ultimately indefinable. A rule-breaker herself, it is impossible to extrapolate rules from her practice: 'the power is in the peculiar endowments of the author...it is genius, in contradiction to talent'. Such an assessment suggests the formidable challenge facing women who chose to follow her 'beyond the metaphysics of her sex', and push the Gothic mode still further.

3

Joanna Baillie and
Charlotte Dacre

In 1798, the year after Radcliffe bowed out of the literary scene, a volume was published anonymously with the arresting title *A Series of Plays: In Which It Is Attempted to Delineate the Stronger Passions of the Mind*. The contents did not disappoint. There was an 'Introductory Discourse' outlining not only a grandiose scheme for the analysis of each passion in a paired tragedy and comedy, but also a radical theory for regenerating dramatic writing. The three plays themselves were judged to be masterly; particularly the tragedies, *De Monfort* and *Basil*, focused respectively on the antithetical passions of hate and love (those posited by the philosopher Malebranche as the root passions). The plots had a simplicity and the language a poetic resonance that had long been missing from British drama.

The volume soon aroused intense interest and speculation. Who was the author? The first reviews, in the *New Monthly Magazine* and the *Critical Review*, praised the strength and originality of the writing while assuming that the author was a man. Some thought it might be Walter Scott. Back in Bath, Hester Piozzi recorded that 'a knot of Literary Characters [including Sarah Siddons] met at Miss [Sophia] Lee's House...deciding – contrary to my own judgment – that a *learned man* must have been the author; and I, chiefly to put the Company in a good humour, maintained it was a woman. Merely, said I, because the heroines are *Dames Passées*, and a man has no notion of mentioning a female after she is five and twenty.'[1] The dramatist Mary Berry had received the book incognito from the author, and had stayed up all night reading it, noting in her diary the following year that 'The first question on every one's lips is, "Have you read the series of plays?" Every body talks in the raptures I always thought they deserved of the tragedies, and of the introduction as of a new and admirable piece of criticism'.[2] She too was of the opinion that the author was a woman, 'only because, no man could or would draw such noble and dignified representations of the female mind as Countess Albini and Jane de Monfort. They often make us clever, captivating, heroic, but never rationally superior.'[3] The opinion grew that Ann Radcliffe was the author, trying her powers in a new genre. Mrs Piozzi reported it as fact to one correspondent. A Mrs Jackson spread the rumour, with a detailed list of stylistic evidence; Radcliffe apparently tried and failed to contact her and put a stop to it.

The play *De Monfort* went into production at Drury Lane, with Sarah Siddons and her brother John Philip Kemble in the lead parts, and still the author did not come forward to claim credit and payment. The playbills were silent on the matter. But some time before its theatrical unveiling, Joanna Baillie disclosed her name, and on opening night, 29 April 1800, she attended with a party of friends and relations. One critic described in retrospect the astonishment caused by the revelation of her authorship:

> The curiosity excited in the literary circle, which was then much more narrow and concentrated than at present; the incredulity, with which the first rumour that these vigorous and original compositions came from a female hand, was received; and the astonishment, when, after all the ladies who then enjoyed any literary celebrity had been tried and found totally wanting in the splendid faculties developed in those dramas, they were acknowledged by a gentle, quiet and retiring young woman, whose most intimate friends, we believe, had never suspected her extraordinary powers.[4]

It is a literary Cinderella story, in which the heroine goes to the ball and lives happily ever after. In spite of recent misguided attempts by some feminist critics to represent Baillie as an oppressed and marginal writer, the fact is that she went on to a highly productive publishing career, a career met with continuous acclaim, and crowned by the appearance of her collected poems and plays in 1851, just before her death aged 88.[5] She had a large circle of friends including some of the most prominent cultural figures of the day. Maria Edgeworth, Anna Laetitia Barbauld, Walter Scott, Lord and Lady Byron, Wordsworth, and Southey, were among her ardent admirers. If her work came

Fig. 5. Engraving of Joanna Baillie from an original portrait by Masquerier.

under attack from the notoriously severe pen of Francis Jeffrey at the *Edinburgh Review,* assassin of *Lyrical Ballads,* then it has to be said she was in excellent company.[6] Her sex was neither a barrier to success and celebrity, nor a shield against serious criticism. Her exceptional literary status, transcending conventions of gender, rested on a tradition which by now included the outstanding examples of Siddons and Radcliffe: women who displayed genius through rule-breaking and the imaginative flights characteristic of Gothic.

Joanna Baillie was born in 1762. Her father was a Presbyterian minister who became professor of divinity at the University of Glasgow before dying in 1783. The Baillies were descendants of the Scottish patriot Sir William Wallace. Her mother was the sister of the famous surgeon Dr William Hunter, who at his death left his London practice and property to Joanna's brother, Matthew. In 1784 Joanna travelled south to join him with her mother and elder sister Agnes. When Matthew married, the Baillie women set up independently in Hampstead, where Joanna and Agnes were to remain until the end of their long lives.

As a child at boarding school Joanna had excelled in music, drawing, mathematics and theatrical improvisations. A birthday poem addressed to Agnes recalls how she discovered her skill for story-telling through the pleasure of evoking fear and wonder in her sister, an eager auditor:

> Thy love of tale and story was the stroke
> At which my dormant fancy first awoke,
> And ghosts and witches in my busy brain
> Arose in sombre show, and motley train.
> This new-found path attempting, proud was I,
> Lurking approval on thy face to spy,
> Or hear thee say, as grew thy roused attention,
> 'What! is this story all thine own invention?'[7]

Her first publication was a book of poetry which appeared in 1790 but went almost unnoticed. Already, though, it showed her interest in the study of human nature and the influence on the mind of contrasting passions. The subtitle explains that the poems will illustrate 'the Different Influence Which the Same Circumstances Produce on Different Characters' and there is a series of 'Addresses to the Night' by 'A Fearful Mind', 'A Discontented Mind', 'A Sorrowful Mind' and 'A Joyful Mind'.[8]

PASSION IN THE PRESENT TENSE

Baillie's tragedies, particularly *De Monfort* and *Orra*, have been discussed as examples of Gothic writing in a number of critical studies.[9] Some of the settings are indeed strongly reminiscent of Radcliffe: the woods by night in *De Monfort*, with a requiem sounding faintly from an isolated convent; the castle in *Orra*, the haunt of outlaws under cover of strange legends, riddled with secret passages, its chambers furnished with locks on the outside. But in terms of plot, they represent an inversion of Reeve and Radcliffe's technique of encrypting homicidal passion in the distant past, and a decisive rejection of the tragicomic structure which permitted the redemption of evil. The contrast should perhaps even be understood as polemical. The trappings of Radcliffe-romance are included by Baillie only to emphasize their essential irrelevance: the real drama is all in the mind. Baillie refuses to buffer the tortured scenes she represents. This is passion in the present tense, as it had also appeared in Lee's *The Recess*, but in Baillie it is simplified and refined to achieve the transparency of a theorum. The remarks of Joseph Donohue regarding Baillie's conception of dramatic character are especially resonant: 'Gothic drama, beginning with Home's *Douglas*, placed special emphasis on an event that took place years before and continues to exert its effects thereafter. *De Monfort* internalizes this convention by redefining it as a mental process in which an evil passion inexplicably takes root in the fallow soul of man and slowly chokes away his life force.'[10]

This experiment bears some relation to Lewis's *The Monk*, as an illustration of the corrosive effect of lust on the character of Ambrosio. The *Plays on the Passions*, as they are generally called, made an important contribution towards the opening up of new possibilities within Gothic writing, as a now-familiarized audience looked for ever-stronger sensations. Future Gothic writers – Charlotte Dacre, Charles Brockden Brown, Mary Shelley, Edgar Allan Poe – would follow this direction of interiorized Gothic.

Baillie's 'Introductory Discourse' from the 1798 volume of plays provides a theoretical basis for the externalized spectacle of inner passions. Wittily, she frames the discussion in terms of the ruling passion of the reader. We are all, she claims, driven to

89

poetry and fiction by curiosity about human nature. We want to go beyond the official accounts of history writing, penetrate the private space of the home and, further, to enter into the minds of others and rummage among their secret desires and motives. We can be diverted for a while by images of the marvellous in romance, or the artifices of sentimental fiction, or the pleasures of epic and pastoral verse, but the 'great master-propensity' for authentic pictures of nature will always reassert itself. Our curiosity about 'beings like ourselves' must be fed if we are to lend a work of literature our 'sympathetick interest'. Nowhere is this rule more applicable than in drama: pared down as it is to dialogue, if the characters do not speak from nature, then the author can offer no compensating distractions. The study of human nature and the persuasive depiction of character – which Baillie terms 'characteristick truth' – are crucial to the dramatist's art.

Baillie represents the taste for tragedy as something universal and primitive. Tragedy is the 'first-born' of dramatic genres, for a number of reasons. In addition to catering to the 'natural inclination' for 'scenes of horrour and distress, of passion and heroick exertion', tragedy permits the maximum exercise of curiosity and sympathy. In tragedy we are permitted behind the scenes into the lives and minds of 'heroes and great men', normally only glimpsed from afar. And in tragedy we see those extremes of conflict and suffering which most powerfully engage our feelings. At this point Baillie introduces the ultimate purpose of tragedy (now personified as a female muse), which doubles as a sketch of her own innovative theatrical practice:

> to her only it belongs to unveil to us the human mind under the dominion of those strong and fixed passions, which seemingly unprovoked by outward circumstances, will from small beginnings brood within the breast, till all the better dispositions, all the fair gifts of nature are borne down before them. Those passions which conceal themselves even to the dearest friend; and can, often times, only give their fulness vent in the lonely desert, or in the darkness of midnight. For who hath followed the great man into his secret closet, or stood by the side of his nightly couch, and heard those exclamations of the soul which heaven alone may hear, that the historian should be able to inform us? and what form of story, what mode of rehearsed speech will communicate to us those feelings whose irregular bursts, abrupt transitions, sudden pauses, and half-

uttered suggestions, scorn all harmony of measured verse, all method and order of relation?

No wonder Baillie's contemporaries were riveted by her vision. It is both alluring and intensely sinister. The passions are constructed as an inexplicable fatality, divorced from social context, unfolding with an irresistible autonomous force, pent up within an individual life which it will parasitically devour. And the audience is to be made privy to this horrible spectacle of a soul eaten alive, will eavesdrop on exclamations of isolated torture which only heaven should hear,[11] will be initiated into the language of the unspeakable. The workings of the soul are represented as absolutely private and secret, precisely in order to enhance the pleasure of violation and absolute public exposure in the name of 'sympathy' and knowledge.

In a study of this length, it is not possible to explore very far the social resonances of Baillie's poetics, though it is easy enough to identify certain ideological affinities. Baillie brilliantly refashions tragedy along Gothic lines for an age of possessive individualism and state surveillance. Her theatre most closely resembles Jeremy Bentham's panopticon, the ideal prison, in which the perfect visibility of the prisoners by an unseen eye stands, according to Michel Foucault's well-known account, as a general model for relations of power in the modern liberal state. But the baleful cast of her ideas has been obscured in recent criticism, by a determination to take the stress on sympathetic identification as a cosy, feminine alternative to 'patriarchal' tragic practice. Attempting to set up Baillie as a feminist sacred cow does her no favours. There is nothing cosy about her tragedies nor the response to them demanded of the viewer. Like the other writers discussed in this book, she was determined above all to make her mark in the literary world, and was willing to use the most powerful – the most ideologically arresting – means to do so. Issues of gender play a part in this ambition. But Baillie was intent on demonstrating her ability as a woman to rival men in the display of genius, not on defining an alternative feminine aesthetic. Harriet Martineau spoke of cherishing Baillie's memory for the 'invulnerable justification which she set up for intellectual superiority in women'.[12]

In the 'Introductory Discourse', there is an interesting shift in the gender of personal pronouns relating to dramatic writing. At first, when Baillie discusses the primary concerns of the dramatist, she refers to 'him' and 'his' works. At a later stage, as she warms to her argument, tragedy (it has already been noted) is personified as a 'she', who puts into effect 'her' various techniques, including the innovations cited above. Personification is a common enough device in aesthetic discussion of the time, but here, given the sex of the author which would be revealed in the third edition of 1800, there is a fortuitous merging of art and artist, equivalent to Sarah Siddons's representation as the Tragic Muse. There is a subliminal message asserting women's capacity for representing and embodying tragic passion, reinforced by a statement in a footnote:

> I have said nothing here with regard to female character, though in many tragedies it is brought forward as the principal one of the piece, because what I have said of the above characters is likewise applicable to it. I believe there is no man that ever lived, who has behaved in a certain manner, on a certain occasion, who has not had amongst women some corresponding spirit, who on the like occasion, and every way similarly circumstanced, would have behaved in the like manner.

But Baillie goes much further than simply claiming her place among tragedians. The overall purpose of the 'Discourse' is a critique of the entire dramatic inheritance in tragedy and comedy, condemnation of tired imitation in contemporary practice, and a call for bards possessing 'strong original genius' to point the way back to truth and nature. It goes without saying that the author herself must be numbered among this elite. While she is appropriately modest as a neophyte, she also has the courage of her convictions: 'I am emboldened by the confidence I feel in that candour and indulgence, with which the good and enlightened do ever regard the *experimental efforts* of those, who wish in any degree to enlarge the sources of pleasure and instruction amongst men'. Innovation is her *raison d'être*. Her manifesto is not bolstered by didacticism. Indeed, she rebukes tragic poets who have been led away from analysis of the passions by 'a desire to communicate more perfect moral instruction'. The benefit of tragedy should derive from 'the enlargement of our ideas in regard to human nature': a knowledge of the self, which may indirectly lead to moral improvement.

The project Baillie outlined publicly at the age of 36 lasted almost a lifetime. In the course of her prolific career she produced three volumes of *Plays on the Passions* – ten plays in all – and thirteen other plays, not to mention numerous poems. Bertrand Evans has proposed that ten of the tragedies can be categorized as Gothic drama: *Orra, The Dream, Henriquez, Romiero, Ethwald* (in two parts), *De Monfort, Rayner, The Family Legend, The Separation,* and *Witchcraft.*[13] I will be discussing only two of them, already mentioned: *De Monfort* (1798), by far the best known of her works then and now, and *Orra* (1812), which Evans claims best illustrates 'Miss Baillie's "Gothicity"'.[14]

Kemble's rapid determination to bring *De Monfort* to the stage of Drury Lane, in spite of the play's anonymity, has already been mentioned. It is unsurprising, given the fact that the play might have been written as a vehicle for himself and Siddons. Baillie's nephew suggested that the characters of De Monfort and his elder sister Jane were indeed intended as portraits of the two actors.[15] For Kemble, the role of a man of fine qualities driven to murder by an irrational hatred presumably reflected his talents as an interpreter rather than his actual personality. But in the case of Jane De Monfort, a woman who has nobly sacrificed her life to the duty of caring for her orphaned siblings, but who is still capable of enthralling every man she meets with her beauty and bearing, the terms in which she is praised in the play unquestionably echo descriptions of Siddons.[16] She is 'A noble dame, who should have been a queen' (*DM* I. i. 5); 'So stately and so graceful is her form', comments a servant, 'I thought at first her stature was gigantic' (*DM* II. i. 10–11): the awe she inspires is almost supernatural, as is her ability to turn all around her into willing slaves. It is understandable that Siddons requested Baillie to 'write me more Jane De Monforts'. The production only lasted for eleven performances and there are mixed reports of its reception,[17] but Siddons chose it for her benefit on 5 May 1800, acted the role again in Edinburgh in 1810 with her son Henry as De Monfort, and continued to use the play in recitations.[18]

The plot takes the novel form of a perverse love triangle, without romantic love. De Monfort is monomaniacally attached to Rezenfelt through his hatred, and there are homoerotic undercurrents in their interaction. Jane, De Monfort's sister, who raised him after the death of their mother, attempts to draw him away from this hate by appealing to their mutual love, which itself has a focused intensity verging on the incestuous. The addition of a third current, an unfounded rumour mentioned in passing that Rezenfelt and Jane are secretly in love, produces a short-circuit in De Monfort's mind that leads to murder. He waylays Rezenfelt in the woods outside the town and savagely stabs him to death.

The context for the drama is deliberately vague. The initial stage direction sets the scene as simply 'a town in Germany'. At the outset we learn that De Monfort has left his home to return to the town where he once lived. He is moody and irascible, yet his servants are loyal, and a friend, Count Freberg, who hurries to greet him, bears witness to his previously amiable nature. A first aside from De Monfort to the audience, however, signals a radical disaffection from his surroundings. The second scene develops suspense, as indications of De Monfort's pathology emerge, through symptom (he wrecks a room at the very mention of Rezenvelt), and the image of an incommunicable interiority. He taunts Freberg for his attachment to social surfaces and inability to penetrate the depths of human nature:

> That man was never born whose secret soul,
> With all its motley treasure of dark thoughts,
> Foul fantasies, vain musings, and wild dreams,
> Was ever open'd to another's scan.

(DM I. ii. 96–8)

The play's concern with the distance between workable social conduct and the tangled depths of selfhood is shown thematically through numerous references to clothing and masks. Flimsy, changeable garments, often inappropriately worn, metaphorize the thin layer of public seeming, a fragile membrane that if severed, would enable the passions to pass freely from subjective confinement into violent reality. The anxiety provoked by this idea finds relief only in the figure of Jane, who represents an ideal of transparent meaning, a seamless union of nature and appearance. And yet Jane is chiefly responsible for the disastrous release of De Monfort's hatred.

In a key episode in the second scene of Act II, Jane forces her brother to confess his feelings. Impervious to his attempted

94

defence of his 'secret troubles', his 'secret weakness', she applies every weapon of emotional blackmail. De Monfort agrees at last to 'tell thee all – but, oh! thou wilt despise me./For in my breast a raging passion burns,/To which thy soul no sympathy will own –' (*DM* II. ii. 8–10). And so it transpires: Jane is horrified and uncomprehending. Threatened with rejection, De Monfort agrees to meet Rezenfelt and be reconciled with him, an action which will only result in an escalation of their animosity. The problem is that De Monfort did not – could not – 'tell all'. The intensity of his hatred is not proportionate to the identifiable cause: Rezenfelt's habit of covertly goading him while pretending friendship. It is the nature of a ruling passion to be monstrous, autogenic, incommunicable. In De Monfort's case it grows to overpower one of his other prime characteristics, pity.

The audience is called upon to wonder as they witness the hero's deterioration, rather than to understand it in logical terms. As a bridge, there is the more homely yet comparable spectacle of the Countess Freberg's envy of Jane, exacerbated by the latter's kindly condescension. But from the final scene of Act IV through the final Act, as the drama grows wilder it is shifted to the appropriate setting of a wood where 'Foul murders have been done, and ravens scream;/And things unearthly, stalking through the night,/Have scar'd the lonely trav'ller from his wits' (IV. ii. 223–5), and to a lonely convent which stands in it. The 'thickly-tangled boughs' provide the obvious correlative for De Monfort's state of mind as he stalks his victim, and the old Gothic convent where he is brought, frozen with horror, after committing the act, is a monument to isolation. Jane arrives, once again shattering his solitude, and endeavouring to fix his mind on prayer and redemption. But the failure of communication – Jane: 'What means this heavy groan?' De Monfort: 'It has a meaning' – sums up the strange confusion of the scene as he, shackled by officers of justice, quickly expires of an internal haemorrhage. In Baillie's original version the peculiar non-event of De Monfort's death occurs off-stage, as if this reverse of a *coup de théâtre* were designed to taunt the audience, with its penchant for predictable shock-tactics. When Edmund Kean restaged the play in 1821, at the urgent request of Byron,[19] at least two important revisions were introduced. De Monfort's hatred was motivated by a love rivalry with Rezenfelt, and De Monfort was

95

brought on-stage to die. These changes help to indicate the originality, the troubling strangeness, of the original version.[20]

'A MIDNIGHT IN THE BREAST'

De Monfort's collapse and death are brought about partly by remorse, partly by sheer horror at the nature of the act he has committed, and specifically, superstitious fear at being left alone with the corpse of his victim. An early poem, 'The Ghost of Edward', dealt with the fanciful horrors that attack the mind. There is 'a midnight in the breast': in this instance also, fear is exacerbated by guilt.[21] Fear of the supernatural – in isolation from any causal factors – was the passion Baillie determined to explore at full length in a tragedy from her last volume of *Plays on the Passions* published in 1812, *Orra*. Set in the late fourteenth century in Switzerland, it concerns the machinations in the household of Count Hughobert, where his ward, the heiress Orra, is being pressured to marry Hughobert's son, Glottenbal, while also being wooed by a young nobleman of reduced fortunes, Theobald. The plot may sound conventional but the heroine is not. She wants to marry no one and live independently (there is some slight mention of charitable works), and manages to persuade Theobold to be her friend rather than her lover. She is not especially beautiful (Theobold: 'to speak honestly,/I've fairer seen', I. i. 129–30), and her character is a composite of mirth and dread, as if Annette, Emily's servant from *The Mysteries of Udolpho*, had usurped the lead role. Romantic love is displaced, as it was in *De Monfort* and in many of Baillie's other plays, with the result that expectations are disrupted and it becomes possible to create more interesting and varied parts for women.

Orra adores ghost stories, and this is her downfall. She is not only highly susceptible to fear but also addicted to the sensation:

> Yea, when the cold blood shoots through every vein:
> When every pore upon my shrunken skin
> A knotted knoll becomes, and to mine ears
> Strange inward sounds awake, and to mine eyes
> Rush stranger tears, there is a joy in fear.
>
> (II. i. 170–75)

Her chief resource to feed her passion is Cathrina, one of her attendants, who has an inexhaustible supply of supernatural legends. But Cathrina is in the power of Rudigere, an illegitimate relation of the count's who plots to marry Orra in order to improve his fortunes. Cathrina has been his mistress and borne his child, and, to save her reputation, she enters into Rudigere's plot to have Orra removed to an ancient castle rumoured to be haunted. There he will use Orra's fear to blackmail her into a union with Glottenbal (he tells the count), but in fact with himself. Theobold learns of the conspiracy, and plans to rescue her by impersonating the spirit of the place, a spectre huntsman. But a message forewarning her goes astray, and terror at his ghostly appearance drives her into a state of derangement, from which, it seems, she will not recover. A repentant Hughobert arrives on the scene with his family, and the villainous Rudigere kills both himself and his rival, the obtuse Glottenbal.

As in the case of *De Monfort*, the relation of *Orra* to an emergent Gothic genre is not straightforward. The play is a medley of familiar tropes: the haunted castle with a story of murder attached to it, riddled with secret passages (cf. almost any Gothic novel from *Castle of Otranto* onwards); the band of outlaws who use the castle as a hide-out under cover of supernatural rumour (cf. *The Mysteries of Udolpho*, Charlotte Smith's *The Old Manor House*, and many others); the noble outlaw chief (a childhood friend of Theobald, who lends his assistance; cf. Schiller, and Dacre's *Zofloya*); the heroine kept in a bedchamber with locks on the outside only (*Mysteries of Udolpho* etc.); the ballad tradition of elopement with a phantom lover (Bürger's 'Lenore', and its variants); the rescue involving impersonation of a phantom lover which ends in disaster (cf. the Bleeding Nun episode from *The Monk*). Indeed, the play's generic knowingness might lead one to imagine that its purpose was solely critical, even satirical. It is worth bearing in mind that two of the best-known burlesques of Gothic were published soon after: E. Stannard Barrett's *The Heroine* in 1813 and Jane Austen's *Northanger Abbey* in 1818. Certainly it is true to say that the devices included by Baillie are more or less stripped of affect: the supernatural is explained so far in advance that the audience is in no danger of falling in with Orra's delusions. But on the other hand, neither is the viewer permitted the security of detached criticism. Baillie maintains sympathetic identification with the heroine throughout the play by showing her insight into her own situation, her courageous resistance to oppression, and her inner struggle against fear. The catharsis of terror for the audience comes with the final scene, and the pitiful spectacle of Orra surrounded by mind-forged monsters.

Orra's passion for fear is not blamed. Like De Monfort's hatred it is something inexplicable and irresistible, an inner sublime. Baillie clearly indicates in her characterizations that possession of a powerful ruling passion is an index of greatness of soul; but it also creates an imbalance which is ultimately self-destructive. It opens De Monfort to criminality, and Orra to victimage. The audience is not called upon to judge and condemn, but rather to lend their understanding and, at the same time, to wonder at these human meteors and derive a vicarious thrill from their disastrous fates. As in all Gothic writing, the purpose of instruction is a fig-leaf; the fundamental pleasure is amoral. Baillie's methods reflected and facilitated the shift of Gothic away from the conventions which had been associated with the earlier phase of experimental supernaturalism and were thus becoming redundant, to the surer foundations of an inner landscape. Passion itself becomes the plot, but unmotivated, reified, an object of fascination in its own right. It would be inappropriate as well as anachronistic to call this *psychological* drama. The diseases of the mind are not submitted to logic. The increase of knowledge may be Baillie's expressed aim, but it is knowledge of an unabashedly corrupt and disingenuous kind, combining the pleasure of unveiling with the retention of some ultimate mystery.

Discussion of Baillie's drama has almost always excluded mention of her poetry, but she was a well-regarded and frequently anthologized poet as well. Her choice of subject matter and form was wide-ranging, but includes a number of supernatural ballads which Orra would have appreciated. Her *Metrical Legends of Exalted Characters* was said to have brought her £1,000 from the publishers Longman,[22] and went through two editions in the year of publication, 1821. 'The Ghost of Fadon', from this volume, is based on a legend concerning William Wallace, a distant ancestor of Baillie.[23] Here, in contrast to the plays, the supernatural is manifestly public. Not only does the ghost appear to a whole company of soldiers, but he challenges Wallace to a duel, and physically blocks him when he tries to escape, eventually presiding over the burning of the castle where the company had attempted to find shelter after military defeat by the English. He is public, too, in his historical significance. He is the spectre of Fadon, a follower killed by Wallace under suspicion of spying. The haunting suggests that he was wrongfully killed, an omen of bad luck for the nation.

> Day rose; but silent, sad, and pale,
>   Stood the bravest of the Scottish race;
> And each warrior's heart began to quail,
>   When he look'd in his leader's face.

There were a variety of Gothic modes current – several forms of fiction, tragic drama, ballads, odes, prose poems in the manner of Ossian – and Baillie felt no inhibition about testing her powers in more than one. In this poem she flaunts her ability to play on the superstition of her readers, while also signalling her personal investment in nationalist politics.

MARRIED TO THE 'MORNING POST'

'Women (saving Joanna Baillie) cannot write tragedy; they have not seen enough nor felt enough of life for it'; Byron's pronouncement in a letter to Thomas Moore undoes itself. First of all, the example of Baillie thoroughly disproves the second clause: few could have seen less of 'life' – in the sense of material for tragedy – than she. Secondly, as Byron made plain in comments elsewhere, most men who attempted the genre could not in his opinion write tragedy either: 'she [Baillie] is our only dramatist since Otway and Southerne'. Byron is interesting as an observer of women's Gothic, not because he lends the authors literary credibility by his attention, but because even his ingrained sexism could not prevent a genuine admiration from breaking through. This was the case in the wider culture as well. However great the social prejudice against the public display of extreme and violent passion by women, the female pioneers of Gothic carried on regardless. They were not afraid of revealing how much they had 'felt' of life. They knew that such representations would find a market, and demand attention from the reviewers which would not automatically be unfavourable. Although they were exceptional, they acted as beacons marking out the extent of what was possible. Britain in the early nineteenth century was not a patriarchal police state. There may have been a lot of talk about the narrow boundaries of the proper feminine, but it was surprising what a woman writer could get away with, and still die peacefully in the odour of sanctity.[24]

The last remark relates to the amazing career of Charlotte Dacre. Any reader of today whose picture of Regency women's writing is based on Jane Austen will read *Zofloya; or, The Moor* (1806) in a state of wondering disbelief. How is it possible that Austen and Dacre existed in the same universe? How could a woman publish a work which features as its heroine a murderous nymphomaniac who gives her body and soul to the devil disguised as a black servant, and sign her name to it. For to mark the event of the first edition, Dacre cast off her previous pseudonym, 'Rosa Matilda', and stood proudly before the public as the author.

But before looking at the novel for which Dacre is chiefly remembered, and the contemporary reception of it, it is worth looking back over what little is known of her history, and at her earlier manifestion as 'Rosa Matilda', for clues to explain her unrivalled hardihood. There is, for a start, an uncertainty over her date of birth, which is not without interest in itself. Dacre herself was adamant on the point of her age. She declares in the foreword to her two-volume book of poems *Hours of Solitude*, published early in 1805, that she is 23, which would mean that she was born in 1781 or 1782. Throughout the volume she makes special note of poems written before the age of 19 – there are quite a large number of them – including an appendix of verse written between the ages of 13 and 15. The gesture commonly used to soften criticism is here so relentless that it becomes instead overt bragging at her precocious talents. Her first novel, *The Confessions of the Nun of St Omer*, was published in the same year, with a dedication to Matthew Gregory Lewis which states that the book was written at 18 (i.e. around 1798), then put by for a few years. There will be more to say about the significance of Lewis shortly. For now, it is enough to recall that his

Fig. 6. Frontispiece portrait of 'Rosa Matilda' from Charlotte Dacre's *Hours of Solitude* (London, 1805).

controversial bestseller, *The Monk* (1796), was purportedly written at the age of 17 and, like *Confessions*, 'chiefly as a resource against *ennui* and for want of better employment'.[25] Contradicting Dacre's claims, her obituary in *The Times* states that her age at time of death on 7 November 1825, was 53, which would put her birth-date ten years earlier, around 1772. It is not impossible, of course, that the newspaper committed a simple typographic error; no other evidence is currently available. The recent editors of *Zofloya* have adopted the earlier date, but it is important to remember in this case that she has a separate 'authorial' age, for youthfulness is part of her writing persona.

Dacre's origins are obscure, one would say even deliberately concealed. A casual note in a poem by Byron and an obscure volume of verse, *Trifles of Helicon* by Charlotte and Sophia King, dedicated to their father, are all that remains to identify her as the daughter of Jonathan or John King (born Jacob Rey, 1753– 1824) and his wife Deborah Lara.[26] King was a colourful figure, a banker and political radical, who divorced Deborah in 1785 in order to marry Jane Butler, the widow of the second Earl of Lanesborough, and 'gave excellent dinners' according to Byron, attended by such literary figures as Robert Merry, Godwin, Holcroft and Sheridan.[27] Charlotte's sister Sophia went on to publish four novels under her own name.[28] But Charlotte made the decision to relaunch her career under the pseudonym 'Rosa Matilda', a very resonant compound in the late 1790s.

In this decade, newspapers became an important outlet for new poetry: they offered writers a regular income and an audience far wider than most books would receive. Through the 1790s the *Morning Post* was especially prominent, with first Robert Southey then Mary Robinson as literary editors, and Wordsworth and Coleridge among the other contributors. In 1789 the *World* had launched a craze with its introduction of 'Della Crusca', the pseudonym of Robert Merry, who specialized in highly wrought love poetry and drew into poetic dialogue 'Anna Matilda' (poet and dramatist Hannah Cowley), creating for the readers the image of an exciting, ongoing literary love affair. Other writers who joined the Della Cruscan masquerade were Robinson ('Laura Maria') and Robert Stott ('Hafiz'). Charlotte ventured into newspaper verse-writing with a tag suggestive of an intention to supplant Cowley; it is clear she had a competitive instinct. Poems collected in *Hours of Solitude* have the typically flirtatious, dialogic format of the School: 'Eloquence' ('Written at fifteen') is 'Addressed to a gentleman who eloquently maintained that Love, if analysed, was Folly'; 'Passion Uninspired by Sentiment' is 'Addressed to him who denied their existing together'. There are items by male collaborators and interlocutors at the *Morning Herald*, including a gentleman signing himself 'Azor' (*HS* ii. 7–10). The poetry is almost exclusively concerned with the passion of love, covering a spectrum from melancholy through misery to nightmare.

Nightmare is where the further connotations of the name 'Rosa Matilda' come in, echoing Lewis's she-devil Matilda from *The Monk*, who first presents herself as the novice Rosario. Although a number of Dacre's poems have the gently fanciful turn of Radcliffe, the dominant model for her Gothic verse is Lewis, and, beyond him, the seminal German poet Bürger, who had electrified the reading public with the supernatural ballad 'Lenore' (five translations into English in 1795). *The Monk* contained a number of poems which achieved considerable success in their own right. 'The Exile' was thought very fine, and the ballad 'Alonzo the Brave, and Fair Imogine', with its immortal description of the spectre-bridegroom – 'The worms, They crept in, and the worms, They crept out,/And sported his eyes and his temples about' – was reprinted separately, inspiring many parodies and even a ballet. *Tales of Wonder!* (1801?), which Lewis put together with the aid of the young Walter Scott, was jokingly referred to as 'Tales of Plunder', designed to cash in on the public's appetite for sensational verse. It was a compendium of translations and adaptations as well as some original material, and included numerous variations on 'The Water-King' (a Danish ballad Lewis had included in the novel), and a translation of a Bürger poem by Scott. In 1803 there was a performance of a dramatic monologue in verse by Lewis called 'The Captive' which aimed to display the onset of insanity, but it caused such terror among the audience on its first showing that the author withdrew it.[29]

In *Hours of Solitude* Dacre included her own poem called 'The Exile' ('Written at Sixteen' and therefore pointedly before the publication of *The Monk*), several depictions of insanity, two prose effusions in the manner of Ossian, and a number of horror ballads, including a version of a metrical tale of seduction and infanticide by Bürger, 'The Lass of Fair Wone', which she had seen translated in a periodical, and decided to improve on, disliking the 'too familiarly disgustful' methods of the German school (*HS* ii. 83). There is even a parody, 'Grimalkin's Ghost; or The Water Spirits', in which a drowned cat and her litter return to haunt their murderer, 'In humble imitation of the soaring flights of some legendary and exquisitely pathetic modern Bards' (*HS* ii. 60): but if this was aimed at Lewis, it was also emulating him, for he was his own best parodist. Four of the most Gothic poems in the collection were originally published in a romance by another author, *The Fatal Secret* of 1801. They include 'The Skeleton Priest; or, The Marriage of Death', derived from 'Alonzo and Imogine', and 'The Aireal Chorus; or, The Warning', a more original spin on vampirism, with an effective simplicity of diction all too rare in Dacre.

Adriana Craciun has suggested that the most thematically intriguing poetry forms a series, dealing with visitations by phantom lovers of an altogether more subtle and evanescent kind.[30] There are two versions of the apostrophe 'The Mistress To the Spirit of her Lover', the first in the style of Ossian (*HS* ii. 31–3), the second versified (*HS* ii. 34).[31] The mistress questions the existence of the spirit who appears to haunt her, but finally submits to fantasy, madness and death. In terms of structure, the poem pursues undecideable oppositions of visibility and darkness, life and death, the senses and imagination. Rhetorically, the affect is a tease: 'Can I not press thee to my bosom? Oh miserable mockery! thou woulds't evaporate in my embrace'; 'O! Lover illusive, my senses to mock –/'Tis madness presents if I venture to think'. The mistress, yearning for union, is tantalized and in the end seeks the relative certainty of death. Similarly, the reader, bewildered by the mingling of the material and spiritual, is caught in a web of prurient interest. The technique is worth noting, since it is characteristic of all Dacre's narrative fictions apart from *Zofloya*; the poems allegorize the problem, is it love or lust, will it be consummated, or elevated to the region of the spirit? The answer is always disillusioningly – but grippingly – material.

A fascinating variation on this theme is Dacre's highly self-conscious address 'To the Shade of Mary Robinson' (*HS* i. 130–33).

The life of the actress, writer and courtesan Mary Robinson relates to Dacre's own career in many ways. She had died in 1800 at the early age of 42, after many years of ill health arising from partial paralysis of her legs. She had also suffered chronic financial difficulties as a result of high living and gambling. It is as an innocent sufferer that she is addressed in the poem:

> Oh, thou! whose high virtues, angelic, yet glorious,
> At once move my wonder, my pride, and my tears,
> Still, still in the grave dost thou triumph victorious,
> Thy fame sounding loud in thine *enemies'* ears!

This encomium bears witness to the public relations triumph of Robinson's writing persona. During the 1790s, she wrote feverishly to keep her creditors at bay. As a poet (adopting a number of pseudonyms), she was dubbed the 'English Sappho'; as a novelist, she kept on the radical edge of the sentimental norm, raising political issues and pushing against social mores, for instance by sympathetically portraying illegitimacy in *The Natural Daughter*. It has already been mentioned that she was for a time queen of the *Morning Post*, a commissioning editor, and regularly paid to have her enterprises sympathetically reported elsewhere in the press. The young Dacre appears to have hero-worshipped her: there are a couple of poems concerning 'Laura' (Robinson's pseudonym) in the juvenilia. She was not alone. The *Lady's Monthly Museum* (1801) printed an adulatory obituary, but the indignant response of some readers uncovers the other side of Robinson's public image: sexual scandal. This doubleness is well reflected in Dacre's poem. She woos Robinson's high poetic spirit, and leaves her more bodily adventures unmentioned; but surely not unforgotten by the reader. Robinson had attained instant notoriety when she became the mistress of the Prince Regent in 1779–80, and she later pursued a very public ten-year liaison with the military hero Colonel Balastre Tarleton. For Dacre, in the process of creating a persona for herself which combined visionary poetry and sex, association with both sides of Robinson's history would have been welcome. But there was another and closer tie, not previously noted in Dacre's biography. Her own father, John King, was one of Robinson's first lovers, and when he failed to extort money from her in the profitable aftermath of the affair with Prince George, published the kiss-and-tell volume *Letters from Perdita to a Certain Israelite, and His Answers to Them* (London, 1781).[32]

Dacre states in the poem to Robinson that 'I ne'er was so happy thee living to know' (according to her own chronology, she was not yet born when the affair took place). But the girl would surely have heard about the connection, given King's public revelations. In any case, in the year *Hours of Solitude* was published, 1805, she would have had a good deal of fellow feeling with the tarnished angel. She had entered into an affair with the married Nicholas Byrne, owner and editor of the *Morning Post* from 1803 to 1833, and may already have been bearing his child, born the following year and later baptized William Pitt Byrne. Two more followed: Charles, born 1807, and Mary, born 1809. They did not marry until 1815, presumably after the death of Byrne's first wife.[33]

For many years after her death, memory of Dacre was kept alive by a few lines in Byron's satirical poem *English Bards and Scotch Reviewers* (1809):

> Far be't from me unkindly to upbraid
> The lovely ROSA's prose in masquerade,
> Whose strains, the faithful echoes of her mind,
> Leave wondering comprehension far behind.

(ll. 755–58)

The remarks, appearing in a passage which generally dismisses the Della Cruscan newspaper poets, are flattering. Even more so is the footnote: 'This lovely little Jessica, the daughter of the Jew K[ing], seems to be a follower of the Della Cruscan School, and has published two volumes of very respectable absurdities in rhyme, as times go; besides sundry novels in the style of the first edition of the Monk'. In the 1816 edition he added, 'She since married the Morning Post – an exceeding good match'. Why 'an exceeding good match'? Perhaps because Byron knew of her previous compromised status as a mistress with illegitimate children. More likely, though, given the literary context, approval for the pairing of a Della Cruscan survivor with a newspaper hack. A further note was added in pencil to Byron's copy 'and is now dead – which is better', though this may not be in the poet's hand. Better dead? The remark seems gratuitously cruel. Death a better match than Byrne? There might be something in this ... for with *Zofloya* Dacre succeeded in taking a work of popular fiction beyond its transient fate into a twilight zone of immortal infamy, previously inhabited only by 'the first edition of the Monk'.[34]

PASSION UNLIMITED

Dacre's first novel, *Confessions of the Nun of St Omer*, was published in 1805 in the same year as *Hours of Solitude*, and dedicated to M. G. Lewis. She speaks of her admiration for his 'very various and brilliant talents', but disclaims any attempt to imitate his 'style or subject'. It is true that there are no Gothic horrors in the novel, apart from mental torture suffered by the heroine under pressure, and a poem 'The Spectres' Jubilee' (one of several that also appear in the volume of poetry). *Confessions* is essentially a novel of passion, comparable to Mary Hays's *Memoirs of Emma Courtney* (1796) or Mary Wollstonecraft's unfinished *The Wrongs of Woman; or Maria* (1798). As an analysis of the manner in which a young mind becomes prey to excesses of feeling, it is comically inept. But it comes to life in the scenes of the heroine's debates with her libertine admirers. Dacre revelled in the arguments of amoral sensualists. The luxurious deferral of consummation through talk in this manner exemplifies the novel's very literary eroticism. We know the heroine Cazire is doomed to transgress when the philosopher Fribourg whips out his secret weapon: Goethe's novel 'Werter and Charlotte' (*The Sorrows of Young Werther*) (C. 116).[35]

Confessions was a success, going through three editions by 1807. But Dacre was clearly not satisfied. With *Zofloya*; she took on a new name[36] and a new approach, and set out to rival Lewis directly. The novel is a complete departure from the dominant sentimental discourse, displaying instead a steely-eyed intention to shock. Poetry is eliminated as a distraction. One reviewer spoke of being lured to read it by 'the puffs [bought praise] so liberally bestowed by some of the daily prints'.[37] The book courted comparison with *The Monk*, with a clear intention to trump the other work for salaciousness and horror. There is a reversal of sexes in the principal parts; otherwise the circumstances are similar, but heightened. Whereas in *The Monk* the

107

Devil sends only a 'subordinate but crafty spirit' to do his business and ensnare the soul of the monk Ambrosio, in *Zofloya* Victoria is lengthily courted by the Devil himself. In Lewis the tempter is a conventionally beautiful woman, in Dacre he is very unconventionally a magnificent black servant. Ambrosio rapes a delicately beautiful and innocent young girl and quickly kills her when he risks being caught (later discovering that she was his estranged sister). Victoria murders her husband to possess his brother Henriquez, and then, when the latter resists, 'rapes' him (by drugging him). After being again rejected, she revenges herself by hacking to death his fiancée, the fairy-like Lilla, in a protracted scene which reads like a horrific sexual assault, finally throwing the mangled corpse into an abyss out of pure rage.

The reviews almost all dwelt on the comparison, and unsurprisingly almost all condemned Dacre's effort on moral grounds. Most were also dismissive of her literary abilities, ridiculing her management of the narrative, faults in grammar and favourite neologisms like 'enhorrored'. The critic of the *General Review of British and Foreign Literature* (1806) confesses that 'the author tells her tales of indiscriminate horror in many instances with great force' (p. 593). It is certain, at any rate, that the audacity of the attempt earned far more attention and publicity than was normally allotted to a novel.

Dacre was accused of lack of originality, but her anti-heroine Victoria di Loredani, is certainly a remarkable creation. She is described in the opening pages at the age of 15: 'proud, haughty, and self-sufficient – of a wild, ardent, and irrepressible spirit, indifferent to reproof, careless of censure – of an implacable, revengeful, and cruel nature, and bent upon gaining the ascendancy in whatever she engaged' (Z. 4). No concessions are made to the stereotype of the sentimental heroine, yet she remains the centre of narrative interest, with only brief intermissions to examine the progress of her milder brother, Leonardo. In spite of her innate wickedness, there are occasions when she elicits admiration from the narrator and, by extension, from the reader.

At the start of the novel, we are introduced to the family of the Marchese di Loredani as they gather to celebrate Victoria's birthday. In spite of the splendour of their Venetian palazzo, there are seething tensions: the parents married from youthful impulse, and have given little guidance to their own headstrong children. Soon afterwards the marchese's still-beautiful wife, Laurina, is courted and seduced by a guest in their Venetian palazzo, the German libertine Count Ardolph. The guilty couple elope, and Leonardo, from shame, disappears without a word. When the marchese is later killed in a duel with Ardolph, Victoria is taken by her mother to live with the count. Soon, however, Ardolph begins to find her presence tiresome and disposes of the girl by delivering her to the keeping of a puritanical spinster cousin, who inhabits a solitary villa in the countryside.

This imprisonment is the first real test of Victoria's spirit. Distraught at first, and even willing to try one of the elevating pastimes of the Radcliffean heroine, landscape sketching, she soon applies herself to the more practical activities of mimicking obedience to her cousin, and seducing the affections of her servant, Catau. In the end, with a mixture of appeals and threats, Catau is persuaded to swap clothes, and Victoria departs for Venice, penniless and on foot. Her resourcefulness in this episode is impressive, and the narrator notes the 'superior and dignified expression' with which Victoria suppresses her feelings, 'which would have done honour to a nobler motive' (Z. 46).

Back in Venice, she seeks out Berenza, a friend of Ardolph's who had earlier proposed an elopement to her. Berenza is that most dangerous of Dacrean types: the philosophical sensualist, ever ready to ensnare and destroy women with his dazzling arguments and lofty soul. In Victoria, however, he has met his match. Through his eyes, searching for signs of tenderness towards himself, we are persuaded of her unusual charms.

No, her's was not the countenance of a Madona – it was not of angelic mould; yet, though there was a fierceness in it, it was not certainly a repelling, but a beautiful fierceness – dark, noble, strongly expressive, every lineament bespoke the mind which animated it. True, no mild, no gentle, no endearing virtues, were depicted there; but while you gazed upon her, you observed not the want of any charm. Her smile was fascination itself; and in her large dark eyes, which sparkled with incomparable radiance, you read the traces of a strong and resolute mind, capable of attempting any thing undismayed by consequences; and well and truly did they speak. Her figure, though above the middle height, was symmetry itself;

she was as the tall and graceful antelope; her air was dignified and commanding, yet free from stiffness; she moved along with head erect, and with step firm and majestic; nor was her carriage ever degraded by levity or affectation. (Z. 76–7)

In this portrait, Victoria is yet another embodiment of the Siddonian ideal: a Lady Macbeth, a muse of tragedy, resolute, passionate, courageous, a character elevated beyond the limitations of her sex. But the passage is a subtle piece of writing in a text not overburdened with subtlety. It is a fantasy disguised as objectivity, an example of free indirect discourse fusing the delusions of Berenza with the authority of the narrator. On the next page the narrator is able to supply better information: 'Victoria's heart was a stranger to every gentle, noble, or superior feeling' (Z. 77): so much for the transparency of her lineaments.

Yet Victoria appears to fit the bill, and she is able to exploit Berenza's fantasy, since he has indiscreetly betrayed it, telling her that his beloved 'must tower above her sex; she must have nothing of the tittering coquet, the fastidious prude, or the affected idiot: she must abound in the graces of *mind* as well as of *body*' (Z. 75) For a while she attempts to persuade him of the love she does not feel, by imitations of sentimental melancholy (portrayed with a nice comic touch by Dacre). But she only makes sure of him by means of a happy accident which allows her to play the role of tragic heroine to the hilt. Megalena Strozzi, Berenza's jilted mistress, has arranged for an assassin to revenge her. Victoria, lying in bed with her sleeping lover, perceives the intruder and by diverting his dagger thrust, is wounded in the shoulder. Berenza wakes up and the assassin escapes, but not before Victoria recognizes him as her brother.

Berenza is so overcome by her apparent self-sacrifice, that he instantly resolves to marry her. He makes the mistake, however, of explaining that he had not done so before because of her family's disgrace. She had believed her worth to be *sui generis*, and had discounted the question of marriage because her 'boldly organised mind' (Z. 29) shunned convention. Now she is mortally offended, but conceals her feelings. She is biding her time, as she did in her rural imprisonment.

Victoria's passions are unlike anything else in women's Gothic writing of the period. Most Gothic heroines ring the changes between love, fear, joy and grief. In the first half of the novel, this Gothic anti-heroine's soul is dominated, first by pride, then by envy at her mother's happiness with Ardolph, then by hatred and revenge, directed at her mother and later at Berenza. Dacre adds considerably to the emotional spectrum, as if intent on demonstrating the truth of Baillie's contention that women could match any passion felt by men.[38] In most heroines the capacity for strong feeling is allied with a strong imagination, giving rise to a 'genius' for poetry or music. Victoria is without these accomplishments. She has a 'heated imagination' which lends a 'vivid colouring' to her circumstances and surroundings (Z. 28), but her emotions are elemental rather than creative, drawn towards an extraordinary intensity of being, rather than channelled into the social route of aesthetic representation:

> Her's were the *stormy* passions of the soul, goading on to ruin and despair...as the foaming cataract, rushing headlong from the rocky steep, and raging in the abyss below!...The wildest passions predominated in her bosom; to gratify them she possessed an unshrinking relentless soul, that would not startle at the darkest crime. Unhappy girl! whom Nature organised when offended with mankind, and whom education that *might* have corrected, tended only to confirm in depravity. (Z. 78)

In the second half of the novel, the crimes that result from Victoria's 'organization' will come thick and fast. But as the conclusion to this passage suggests the ultimate cause of her passionate criminality remains unclear. Robert Miles, in his reading of the text, has observed that the explanation of her evil nature is overdetermined: divine predestination? bad parenting? the innate selfishness of the 'state of nature' unredeemed by social sentiment?[39] In the opening paragraph of the novel, Dacre seems to echo Baillie in promising to reveal the hidden causes behind events. In fact she keeps the options open, and although perhaps the blame is laid most heavily at the mother's door, Victoria is nevertheless condemned herself for her refusal to forgive Laurina.

Victoria's headlong descent into vice leading to eternal damnation begins with the entrance of Berenza's younger brother Henriquez and his Moorish servant Zofloya. Five years of married life have passed, not happily, but uneventfully. Now Victoria is all of a sudden struck down by a new passion:

111

As though the curse of Laurina were entailed upon her daughter, (that of becoming absorbed by a guilty and devouring flame, with the single exception that, in the case of the former, the heart and mind had been *involuntarily* seduced by a designing betrayer, while the other cherished and encouraged an increasing passion for one who attempted her not, and which common honour should have taught her to repel), Victoria dwelt with unrestrained delight upon the attractions of the object, that had presented itself to her fickle and ill-regulated mind. (Z. 132)

This extraordinary sentence, concerned (as so often) with making and unmaking an etiology of passion, heralds an extraordinary shift. Female lust was a feature of the early part of the narrative and took three forms: there was the licentiousness of Laurina, which, as the narrator observes, was largely passive; in the four chapters devoted to Leonardo's adventures, there was the farcical, unreciprocated lust of the wife of his first patron, Signor Zappi, and the more subtle and successful lust of Megalena, who ensnares her prey to the extent that he will do her murderous bidding. But Victoria's lust is of a different order.[40] We have borne witness to the workings of her mind: up until now, all her passions have centred on herself, and we have seen her capable of remarkable calculation and self-control in order to further them. Lust for the first time makes her vulnerable, irrational, open to frightening fancies; it is a weakness, a fatal flaw, in line with the tragic structure of Dacre's Gothic. Henriquez is devoted to Lilla, his young ward, whom he intends to marry. He ignores Victoria's advances. In frustration she is driven to imagine her first crime, the murder of her husband, and as if in answer to her wish, Zofloya appears, ready to do her bidding.

Dreams begin to determine reality. Victoria dreams of gardens and churches, the intolerable love of Henriquez and Lilla, the splendour of Zofloya, a promise he extorts from her, 'Wilt thou be mine?', the deadly results of her pledge, the natural turned supernatural, strange landscapes traversed with the Moor. She awakens, but the world has become dreamlike too: Zofloya disappears and is said to have been killed, but then miraculously returns; suddenly she sees he is beautiful, she remarks him everywhere, his black skin and dark eyes attract her; in contrast, she is tortured by Lilla's presence, her insistent whiteness and blondeness. Victoria's own body begins to change and take on an alien nature, as she is forced to see herself in the indifferent gaze of Henriquez: ' "Ah! would," cried the degenerate Victoria, "would that this unwieldy form could be compressed into the fairy delicacy of hers, these bold masculine features assume the likeness of her baby face! – Ah! what would I not submit to, to gain but one look of love from the pitiless Henriquez"' (Z. 213–14). As the madness grows, her disorientation is increased by the mesmerizing words of Zofloya, prefixed habitually with 'lovely Signora', 'beautiful Victoria'. Her dependency increases, while he organizes her frustrated passion into acts of violence. The setting has switched to Berenza's isolated mansion in the Apennines, Castella di Torre Alto, perfect for a homicidal house-party. The colour red joins black and white: the red of her blush as she confesses her desire; the red of Berenza's blood when his circulation is tested, spurting out, in a Grand Guignol touch, accusingly in his murderer's face; the blood of Henriquez when he falls on his sword after being tricked into sex with Victoria; the blood of Lilla, red on her flaxen hair.

The showdown between Lilla and Victoria stands out, even amidst the accumulating gore. Percy Bysshe Shelley was to borrow it wholesale, along with much else, in his first attempt at Gothic fiction, *Zastrozzi*. Lilla has previously been abducted by Zofloya and Victoria, and taken out of the way to the remotest part of the mountains, where she is kept chained in a cavern. But after the suicide of Henriquez, Victoria ignores the Moor's instructions to keep her alive, and strides up the mountain bearing a dagger to confront her victim. Lilla, with 'her pale cheek reposing upon her snowy arm', her 'alabaster shoulders', 'polished bosom', and eyes of 'heavenly blue' (Z. 222–3), is the provocative emblem of her failure. ' "Minion! – accursed child!" wildly shrieked the maddened Victoria, "prepare for death!"' (Z. 223) The exchange continues in a welter of dashes and exclamation marks, as Lilla pleads piteously, and Victoria hurls inventive insults. Lilla is dragged to the edge of a precipice, her feet 'left their blood red traces at every step!' (Z. 223). Victoria attempts to stab her, but only cuts her hand. Lilla breaks free and runs, but she is soon recaptured:

Victoria, no longer mistress of her actions, nor desiring to be so, seized by her streaming tresses the fragile Lilla, and held her back. – With her poignard she stabbed her in the bosom, in the shoulder, and other parts: – the expiring Lilla sank upon her knees. – Victoria pursued her blows – she covered her fair body with innumerable wounds, then dashed her headlong over the edge of the steep.– Her fairy form bounded as it fell against the projecting crags of the mountain, diminishing in the sight of her cruel enemy, who followed it far as her eye could reach. (Z. 226)

The scene is a suggestive one for recent critics: it has been read as 'a critique of the female Gothic sublime...as if one of Radcliffe's female subjects, passive, waiting to be penetrated, had her wish literally visited upon her by an avenging member of her own sex'; or as an assault on the ascendant model of femininity, 'The bloody hair and bosom have functioned throughout the entire scene as fetishistic part-objects of the besieged commodity Lilla. To despoil the blond hair and the white bosom of Lilla is to attack the domestic feminine idea at its most potent core – the promise of innocent and nurturing motherhood'.[41] With reference to the contemporary iconography of the passions, the dagger-wielding figure of Victoria was both familiar and estranged. It recalls Lady Macbeth, wresting the daggers from her husband's hands 'to smear/The sleepy grooms with blood', or the counter-revolutionary heroine Charlotte Corday, assassin of Marat. Both the fictional and the historical character were to some extent excused their unfeminine appropriation of the phallic weapon by force of 'high' passion: ambition in the first case, patriotism in the other. Before Corday, the best-known image of a female assassin was undoubtedly a popular engraving of Sarah Siddons in the role of Euphrasia from Arthur Murphy's *The Grecian Daughter*. Paula Backscheider has shown how successive revisions of the picture over the years increased the show of power and resolution in Siddons's pose with uplifted arm and her facial expression, while adding Gothic features to the background (a 1790s version shows a mountain in place of earlier field and trees).[42] Of Siddons's performance, a biographer has noted that 'There was a glorious enthusiasm about her delivery of certain portions. She came to perish or to conquer. She seemed to grow several inches taller', and that the audience 'applauded in rapture for at least a minute' the lines in which she declares her intention to kill the tyrant in the name of liberty.[43] The blow itself she executed as 'an anxious thrust of the dagger ... the unfamiliar weapon glides at the very same moment from her trembling fingers',[44] and she instantly falls at the feet of the father she has saved from harm, her action justified and redeemed by filial piety. Victoria's departure from these models is clear enough. Her attack is motivated by base sexual jealousy and accompanied by exulting cruelty, and this sets her in a different class from the noble Siddonian murderess, and even from M. G. Lewis's variations on the theme.[45]

Dacre's heroine is unique in the Gothic writing of the time: all comparisons simply re-emphasize the unprecedented temerity of the creation. But even Dacre evidently felt the pressure to redeem the display of extreme passion in some way. Even as Victoria comes down from the mountain after the murder, she degenerates into a fearful, imaginative Radcliffean type: 'A certain trepidation of spirits *that she had never before experienced*, caused her to rush along with even greater rapidity, if possible, than she had used in her way thither ... she feared even to turn her head, lest the mangled form of Lilla, risen from the stream, should be pursuing her' (*Z.* 226; emphasis added). Her lust assuaged with human sacrifice, seeking for aid from Zofloya, she reverts to a ghastly facsimile of the dependent little woman, as if she had internalized the spirit of her victim. So incredible, so abnormal, has been her characterization to this point, that the supernatural is able to operate as a *normalizing* factor. Zofloya is fully revealed as a superhuman being, Victoria trembles and submits: their relations, now overtly sexual, mimic a conventionally paternalistic pairing.

The coda of the novel could only be an anticlimax. Victoria's story ends in a cave inhabited by banditti, the chief of whom is found to be her brother Leonardo, with Megalena as his consort. 'Fate' brings Ardolph and the abused and dying Laurina to the same place. The latter's repentant death is followed by Leonardo's swift revenge on Ardolph. Zofloya precipitates the betrayal of the gang to the authorities at Turin, which results in the suicide of Leonardo and his lover, and throws Victoria completely into the Moor's power. She has had twinges of remorse after a dream-visitation from her 'good genius', but now her fate is sealed. She makes a final vow resigning herself wholly to Zofloya; he is transformed into 'a figure, fierce, gigantic, and hideous to behold!' (*Z.* 267), Satan in person, who disposes of her in the manner established by *The Monk*.

The novel closes, as it began, with some cursory moralizing about the need to keep a tight rein on the passions, but it hardly required the elaborate mockery of the reviewers ('if the devil should appear to [young ladies] in the shape of a very handsome black man, they must not listen to him'[46]) to expose the pretence. Dacre appears to have been undeterred by the universal condemnation of her morality in the periodical press. The *Morning Post* (edited by her lover, Byrne), crowed 'where's the male scribbler, with all his pretences,/Like Rosa Matilda, can ravish our senses'.[47] She was well and truly launched as a bestselling author. *The Libertine* (1807), which returns to the formula of *Confessions*, went through three editions in a year. *Zofloya* was pirated in condensed chapbook form as *The Daemon of Venice* in 1810, a sure sign of success, and translated into French in 1812. Her swan song in fiction was *The Passions* (1811), again featuring a female monster; this time a highly cultivated *femme fatale* by the name of Appollonia Zulmer, who plots the corruption of Julie, the pure wife of the man who spurned her. There is a long intermission before the publication of her final work, a poem entitled *George the Fourth* (1822), after which silence, until the obituary in 1825. Much new information about Dacre has come to light as a result of the recent revival of interest in *Zofloya*. It is fairly certain that before long more will be discovered about her eccentric career.

4

Mary Shelley

INHERITANCE AND ORIGINALITY

The Preface to the first edition of *Frankenstein* aims to distance the novel from hackneyed Gothic convention, but in doing so it re-emphasizes one element which, it has been argued here, most crucially characterizes the genre. We are told that the 'event on which this fiction is founded' – the creation of a man from inanimate matter – has been considered by scientific writers 'as not of impossible occurrence'. That is what distinguishes this story, however incredible, from 'a mere tale of spectres or enchantment'. But the Preface then goes on to echo the claim made in the very first 'Gothic story', *The Castle of Otranto*; the claim that by 'creating more interesting situations' than would be allowed in realist fiction, it is possible to examine the ways in which 'mere men and women' would 'think, speak and act' in 'extraordinary positions'.[1] It is this vision of Gothic writing as a laboratory of the mind that is restated and reaffirmed in the Preface to *Frankenstein*:

> The event on which the interest of the story depends...was recommended by the novelty of the situations which it developes; and, however impossible as a physical fact, *affords a point of view to the imagination for the delineating of human passions more comprehensive and commanding than any which the ordinary relations of existing events can yield.* (F. 3; emphasis added)

Mary later was to identify Percy Shelley as the author of the Preface (see F. 197), but this does not discount its value as an authorial statement. Rather, it is salutary in drawing attention to the fact that the view put forward in the Preface was one held in common by her and her associates (notably Percy), and by the writers that most strongly influenced her, who also happened to be her mother and father, Mary Wollstonecraft and William Godwin.

The facts of Mary Wollstonecraft Shelley's life are well known and readily accessible. Rather than reviewing them here in any detail, I want to begin by examining the tributaries of women's Gothic that meet in her work through her familial literary inheritance. Her genealogy is indeed inseparable from her ambitions as a writer. Like many of the women discussed here, she mentions that she 'scribbled' as a child, spending all her free time inventing stories or building castles in the air (F. 192). But the standards of creativity in the Godwin household were remarkable. Her stepsister was to quip, 'In our family, if you cannot wrote an epic poem or novel, that by its originality knocks all other novels on the head, you are a dispicable creature, not worth acknowledging'.[2]

Mary Wollstonecraft, the great political radical and feminist, had died in 1797 giving birth to Mary. She is best known for her advocacy of enlightenment rationalism, and her insistence, in *A Vindication of the Rights of Woman* (1792), that women can and should be equal participants in this ideal. But she was also, privately and publicly, an enthusiast for the passions. Her first novel, *Mary* (1788), counsels calm resignation, while dwelling on the heroine's paroxysms of frustrated love, first for an indifferent female friend, then for a consumptive young man. Wollstonecraft's taste for adventure drew her to Paris, alone, at the moment of Louis XVI's trial and execution. Soon she was living out of wedlock with an American entrepreneur, Gilbert Imlay, pregnant and in hiding from the Terror in a cottage outside Paris. Imlay departed for England, and she soon found she had been deserted. The resulting anguish led to an outpouring of emotion in her letters to him, and two suicide attempts, in spite of her attachment to her infant daughter Fanny.

Settled in London again in 1796 under the name Mrs Imlay, for respectability, she was ready to re-enter liberal intellectual circles, which included such prominent women of the theatre as Elizabeth Inchbald, Mary Robinson, and Sarah Siddons. In her second, unfinished, novel, *The Wrongs of Woman; or Maria* (1798), begun around this time, the heroine-narrator describes her first awareness that she is trapped in a loveless and abusive marriage by identification with the great tragic actress:

Fig. 7. Miniature portrait of Mary Shelley by Reginald Easton.

My delighted eye followed Mrs Siddons, when, with dignified delicacy, she played Calista [in Rowe's *The Fair Penitent*]; and I involuntarily repeated after her, in the same tone, and with a long-drawn sigh,
>'Hearts like our's were pair'd... not matched.'[3]

In the Author's Preface, Wollstonecraft states, 'In writing this novel, I have rather endeavoured to pourtray passions than manners'. Her interest is in the impact of oppressive institutions on the minds of women, rather than in narrative incidents, and she promises 'delineation of finer sensations' than the mere *'stage-effect'* offered by most popular novelists. The novel begins, nonetheless, with a *coup de théâtre*: the heroine inexplicably imprisoned in a lunatic asylum, tormented by memories and fears which drive her to the verge of madness, in the tradition of Lee's Ellinor and Almeyda, Radcliffe's Laurentini, Baillie's Orra, Dacre's Cazire, and a multitude of roles played by Siddons. The opening lines draw precisely the same distinction between supernatural convention and plausible horrors made in the Preface to *Frankenstein*, while, as there, pursuing the Gothic interest in extreme states of mind.

In 1796 Wollstonecraft and William Godwin became lovers, and the following year, when she was six months pregnant, they married. After her death, it was Godwin who edited and published *The Wrongs of Woman* together with other posthumous writings and his memoir of her life. In a Preface to her novel, he mentions that he and a Mr Dyson, the translator of a German Gothic fiction called *The Sorcerer*, were the only friends she had consulted during the writing of it. It is not surprising that she should have turned to Godwin for a response. He was himself the author of a highly successful novel, *Things As They Are; or, The Adventures of Caleb Williams* (1794) in which he had undertaken to examine – in very similar terms – 'the modes of domestic and unrecorded despotism'.[4] He had already published his monumental work of radical philosophy *Enquiry Concerning Political Justice* (1793), which had a huge impact on liberal opinion, but led to Godwin being caricatured in the reactionary press, on the basis of one of his own illustrations, as a desiccated rationalist, who would save Fénelon from a burning building before his own father, because it was for the greater good of mankind. *Caleb Williams* was intended to inject 'interest and passion' into his political arguments.[5]

In the course of his long career as a writer, Godwin continued to explore mental imprisonment and revolt in a series of novels, *St Leon* (1799), *Fleetwood* (1805), *Mandeville* (1817), *Cloudesley* (1830), and *Deloraine* (1833). In 1797 he wrote an unpublished essay entitled 'History and Romance' which serves as a theoretical argument for his literary practice, particularly the earlier novels, those most akin to Gothic. In the present context, the most striking feature of the essay is its uncanny anticipation of the project announced by Joanna Baillie the following year, in the 'Introductory Discourse' to the first volume of *Plays on the Passions*. As part of his promotion of historical romance over 'abstract' history, Godwin insists on the need to delve into the private character of the public figure. 'I am not contented', he says, 'to observe such a man upon the public stage, I would follow him into his closet. I would see the friend and father of a family, as well as the patriot'. Compare Baillie's opening sentence:

> Our desire to know what men are in the closet as well as the field, by the blazing hearth, and at the social board, as well as in the council and the throne, is very imperfectly gratified by real history; romance writers, therefore, stepped boldly forth to supply the deficiency...[6]

Rather than resenting the coincidence, Godwin acknowledged the similarity of their aims. In the Preface to *Mandeville*, he remarked that his tale had been partly inspired by Baillie's play *De Monfort*. Mary Shelley, as we shall see, was herself a diligent student of Baillie's work, and may well have been led to it by her father's call to lay aside 'the generalities of historical abstraction' and 'mark the operation of the human passions'.

In 1814, with the entrance of Percy Bysshe Shelley into her life, came a new delight in flashy Gothic excess, to add to the high-minded Godwinian analysis of the passions. Shelley had spent his adolescence in a fever of novel-reading and experiments with alchemy. His cousin Tom Medwin, a fellow pupil at Syon House prep school, recalled him buying from a local bookseller Radcliffe's *The Italian*, Dacre's *Zofloya*, Lewis's *The Monk*, along with a range of lesser known Minerva Press authors.[7] He quickly turned author himself, writing poems in imitation of Lewis and 'Rosa Matilda', and encouraging his younger sisters to do the same. Some of these were published in

1810 – when he was 17 – at the expense of his indulgent grandfather, under the title *Original Poems by Victor and Cazire*, his sister Elizabeth assuming the name of Dacre's heroine from *Confessions of the Nun of St Omer*. The poems were not so original, though: a direct plagiarism of Lewis led to the whole edition being pulped. Around the same time he was plundering *Zofloya* to produce his first novel, *Zastrozzi*. Any casual survey will reveal the extent of the debt, from the overheated language to the characters and incidents, with the distinction that Shelley's imitation is entirely, rather than occasionally, risible.[8] This and another novel heavily indebted to Dacre and Lewis, *St Irvyne, or The Rosicrucian* were published at the expense of the author in 1810 and 1811. A tale called *The Nightmare* that Shelley wanted Fuseli to illustrate, and a verse drama called *The Wandering Jew* written with Tom Medwin, did not make it into print. He was far more interested in his adventures in the book market than in settling down to study at the University of Oxford. In November 1810 he wrote to the publisher Stockdale regarding *St Irvyne* with the swagger of an experienced literary speculator: 'As to the method of publishing it, I think as it is a thing which almost *mechanically* sells to circulating libraries, etc., I would wish it to be published on my *own* account'.[9] Four months later he was expelled from Oxford for an atheistical pamphlet.

It was as the author of *Zastrozzi* and *St Irvyne* that Shelley introduced himself by letter to Godwin early in 1812. In the latter tale, he had borrowed from *St Leon* the Rosicrucian motif of the 'elixir of eternal life', and it seems to have been by this route that he came to *Political Justice*, and began to abandon Gothic fantasy for more serious political and philosophical pursuits under Godwin's guidance. But still the plots of romance continued to shape his experience and inform his actions, as he first eloped with the schoolgirl Harriet Westbrook, whom he saw as a victim of oppression, and then did the same again three years later with 16-year-old Mary. The second time round, however, the stunt was adulterous, and the resulting scandal was to cast a pall over the lives of everyone concerned.

In the short term, as Percy and Mary escaped to France, accompanied by her even younger stepsister Jane (later known as Claire) Clairmont, the effect of their crime was to draw them defiantly and rapturously together. As they travelled, they began a shared programme of reading, which justified their feelings and gave them a sense of purpose. Works by Wollstone-craft, Shakespeare and Byron, brought by Mary and described by her biographer as an 'emblematic trousseau', sustained them in their six weeks' exile.[10] On returning to London in September 1814 and finding themselves still rejected by their families, their reading became more intensive and varied. The titles were carefully recorded in a journal kept by Mary with occasional contributions from Percy. It is clear that Mary was being submitted to a crash course in the literature of terror. Almost immediately she is consuming, among other things, Veit Weber's *The Sorceror* (we recall that the translator was a friend of her mother), *The Monk*, and Southey's verse tale in the style of *Vathek*, *Thalaba the Destroyer* (Shelley had visited Southey in the winter of 1811). On 10 October Mary read a heady mixture of *Political Justice*, *Zastrozzi*, and works by her mother. On 23 November Percy visited the Minerva Press Library, and Claire and Mary in turn then read *The Italian*. The journal entry for 27 November records: 'Read the Italian & talk all day – a very happy day indeed'.[11] The next month, she embarked on the three volumes of *Plays on the Passions*, which absorbed her – now six months pregnant – every day from 21 to 27 December; so much so, that Percy makes most of the journal entries on these dates.

In France, Percy had begun an orientalist drama called *The Assassins*, Mary, a story titled 'Hate', and Claire, a tale of tortured sensibility, 'The Ideot'. Only Percy continued writing in London, but all three, with the addition of Shelley's friend Thomas Jefferson Hogg, began experimenting with oral story-telling and the cultivation of fear. Claire had already betrayed her talent for fear during readings of Shakespeare's tragedies on their return boat journey through Germany; it is noted in the journal that certain scenes gave her the 'horrors'. On one memorable occasion in October, recorded at length by both Percy and Claire, they talked politics and gossiped until late into the night, after Mary had gone to bed, until Percy, remarking it was the 'witching hour', became 'conscious of an expression in his countenance which he cannot repress', and asked her 'Did you ever read the tragedy of Orra?' The reference to Baillie's drama of a young woman who goes mad with fear provided the necessary cue. Claire retired, but soon gratifyingly burst into Percy and Mary's bedroom: 'Her countenance was distorted most unnaturally by horrible dismay. It beamed with a whiteness that seemed almost like light...her lips & cheeks were of one deadly hue. The skin of her face & forehead was drawn into innumerable wrinkles, the lineaments of terror that could not be contained'. Her eyes were so wide that they looked as though they had been 'newly inserted in ghastly sport in the sockets of a lifeless head'. He took her out and engaged her in more 'awful conversation' – for though they tried to talk on other topics, they kept coming back to 'these mysteries' – until Claire 'shrieked and writhed on the floor', and Mary had to be called in to calm her.[12] On another occasion Hogg came and related his supernatural experiences, periodically interrupted by Claire's 'childish superstition'.[13] Although Mary's part in these incidents was limited, she read Percy's accounts in the journal, and could not help but observe the techniques being tested on her stepsister, the very model of a susceptible reader of Gothic.

These midnight séances look forward to the famous ghost-story 'competition' at the Villa Diodati near Geneva which gave birth to *Frankenstein*. After a year and a half in England, during which Mary lost her first, premature baby, bore another, William, and married Percy following the suicide of Harriet, they set out for the continent, again accompanied by Claire. By Lake Geneva they met Lord Byron, who had begun a desultory affair with Claire in London, and was willing to make the acquaintance of Shelley, as the author of *Queen Mab*. On the wild stormy night of 16 June, the Shelleys gathered with Byron and his personal physician John Polidori, and read aloud from a book of tales of terror, *Fantasmagoriana, ou Recueil d'histoires d'apparitions de spectres, revenants, fantômes, etc.* Byron proposed that they write stories of their own, and told Mary, 'You and I will publish ours together'.[14] The next morning, Percy and Byron began their tales, while Polidori and Mary floundered. Much later, she gave an account of this moment as a crisis of authorship.

> I busied myself *to think of a story*, – a story to rival those which had excited us to this task. One which would speak to the mysterious fears of our nature and awaken thrilling horror – one to make the reader dread to look round, to curdle the blood, and quicken the beatings of the heart. If I did not accomplish these things, my ghost

124

story would be unworthy of its name. I thought and pondered – vainly. I felt that blank incapability of invention which is the greatest misery of authorship, when dull Nothing replies to our anxious invocations. 'Have you thought of a story?' I was asked each morning, and each morning I was forced to reply with a mortifying negative. (F. 195)

She was threatened not only by immediate comparison with two writers she regarded as great geniuses of the age, but also by the burden of the whole Gothic tradition, now fifty years old. What resources could she find to surpass the horror literature she had studied so assiduously? How could she arouse the passion of fear, a skill regarded in her circle as an ultimate test of imaginative power?

She went on to describe how – stimulated by conversation about experiments in galvanism and the possibility of reanimating a corpse – she retired to bed, closed her eyes (though she did not sleep), and like a more passive Lady Macbeth, allowed the forces of darkness to take over her mind. 'My imagination, unbidden, possessed and guided me, gifting the successive images that arose in my mind with a vividness far beyond the usual bounds of reverie'. She saw a succession of scenes in which the scientist gives life to 'the hideous phantasm of a man', and then flees in terror. He tries to find escape in sleep, but awakes to see his creature standing by the bedside 'looking on him with yellow, watery, but speculative eyes' (F. 196). Mary's own terror convinced her that she had found her story.

With the encouragement of Percy, she began to expand the short tale into a novel, though she was to emphasize that 'I certainly did not owe the suggestion of one incident, nor scarcely of one train of feeling, to my husband' (F. 197). The setting in and around Geneva became important. A visit to Chamonix high in the Alps was incorporated; the desolate Mer de Glâce was made the scene of the creature's reunion with his maker, when he recounts the miseries of his solitary life. Work continued on return to England in September. While Shelley spent time in London on business, Mary settled with the rest of the family in Bath for four months. Emily Sunstein has remarked that Bath with its 'complacent English norms' seems 'a curious backdrop for her blasphemous story'.[15] But as we have seen, the city had nurtured the talents of three of the most influential figures of women's Gothic: Sarah Siddons, Sophia Lee, and Ann Radcliffe. Mary may have been vaguely aware of it. The beautiful closing line of *Frankenstein* – 'He was soon borne away by the waves, and lost in darkness and distance' – was adapted from Lee's *The Recess*, and could be taken as a homage (see above p. 48).

CREATIVE FLUX

The endurance of *Frankenstein* and the mutations of its monster – film icon, breakfast cereal, figure of speech – has been the subject of a number of studies. Even more attention has been devoted to its multifarious literary, political, philosophical and scientific sources, a tribute to Mary Shelley's voracious reading habit; with claims made for the centrality of works from Milton's *Paradise Lost* (signalled by Shelley herself in the epigraph, and numerous references and allusions) to Humphry Davey's *Elements of Chemical Philosophy* (1812), and the obscure feminist romance *The Empire of the Nairs* (1811) by James H. Lawrence.[16] It is impossible here to comment usefully on the enormous secondary literature concerning the novel and its legacy, let alone do justice to the critical debate, though some guidance will be offered in the Bibliography. My purpose in this chapter is simply to locate Shelley's writings in the particular field of interests I have called 'women's Gothic'. That is to say, the focus remains on the author's claim to imagination, genius, originality, and on her aim to represent and transmit powerful emotion in a way which, at the same time, responds to the demands and opportunities of the marketplace.

I have outlined Shelley's extensive knowledge of the Gothic tradition, and suggested that observation of the passions was both a political and an aesthetic imperative in her immediate circle. She could not have the same freedom to experiment as Reeve, Lee or Radcliffe, unconscious that their personal determination to make a mark on the literary scene was helping to forge a distinct genre. Through the late 1790s and the first decade of the nineteenth century, Joanna Baillie and Charlotte Dacre responded to the saturation of the market for terror with escalation of affect, greater leaps of imagination, increasing disregard for moral stricture, extremes of passion designed to touch the audience with unprecedented force. The repertoire of skeletons and spectres that had stood the Gothic pioneers in such good stead, had been effectively made redundant by M. G. Lewis's excesses. Ambitious writers like Baillie and Dacre had to seek out novel sources of terror. This was the problem Shelley also faced, as a belated contender. In the following account of her first novel, I will refer to the edition published in 1818 (now readily available in paperback) rather than the revised 1831 edition, because it is the truer index of the literary concerns of the moment.

Like all innovative successes *Frankenstein* was both deeply familiar to its original audience, and shockingly new. One aspect of its familiarity was the conflict between passion and sentiment, a form of dramatization that can be traced through the history of Gothic from *Otranto* onwards. On the one hand, the ruling passion that elevates, isolates and torments; on the other, the gentle sentiment which binds one individual to another, nurturing and comforting. In Shelley's novel these two principles are bleakly, even programmatically, opposed. Frankenstein, as a child raised in the bosom of a loving family, and as a student of natural philosophy at the University of Ingolstadt, displays a genius which sets him apart. We are told, from the start of his narration, that natural philosophy is 'the genius that has regulated my fate': a spirit that has possessed him (*F.* 22). As a boy he read obsessively in volumes of the old alchemists, because they promise greatness, the discovery of the philosopher's stone or the elixir of life; he is disgusted by modern science with its petty empiricism. When he is converted to chemistry by one of his teachers it is because he is assured that modern philosophers 'have indeed performed miracles': 'They penetrate into the recesses of nature...They ascend into the heavens...They have acquired new and almost unlimited powers; they can command the thunders of heaven, mimic the earthquake, and even mock the invisible world with its own shadows' (*F.* 30–31). Now Frankenstein becomes legendary for his application and skill: 'My ardour was indeed the astonishment of the students; and my proficiency, that of the masters' (*F.* 32). After two years he begins to investigate the 'principle of life', until a 'brilliant and wondrous' light breaks upon him: 'I was surprised that among so many men of genius, who had directed their inquiries towards the same science, that I alone should be reserved to discover so astonishing a secret' (*F.* 34). After another two years of superhuman effort, he has created the body of a man to which he can gift life.

To this god-like achievement, he sacrifices ties of affection and family duty. With hindsight, he accepts blame: the human ideal is 'a calm and peaceful mind' untroubled by 'passion or a transitory desire'; if any pursuit 'has a tendency to weaken your affections' then it is 'certainly unlawful, that is to say, not befitting the human mind' (*F.* 37). Shelley's stroke of brilliance was to embody this somewhat prosaic moralizing literally. The inhuman passion of Frankenstein will give birth to a non-human being. The being is definitively alienated from human society – more absolutely solitary than any figure yet to appear in Gothic writing, and therefore unrivalled in his lawlessness. Victoria in *Zofloya* is a moral monster, whose only bond of sympathy is with the Devil. But Shelley succeeded in taking the horrifying consequences of criminal desire a step further, by representing a 'real' monster as its actualization. The point that the monster is an extension of Frankenstein, that they are essentially doubles, has been made many times, but it is reinforced when the device is seen as an overreaching attempt by Shelley herself to trump precursor texts.

Frankenstein almost always refers to his creation as a 'daemon', rarely as a 'monster', supporting the idea that it is metaphysically 'other', an emanation of the soul – his soul – rather than a living creature in its own right. At the same time, its hideous physicality is repeatedly emphasized: shrivelled yellow skin, watery eyes, black lips, massive and distorted frame. Physical and metaphysical come together in the creature's insensibility to the elements, and superhuman speed and strength. The latter are the qualities which allow it to elude the destructive purpose of the remorseful Frankenstein, and double back on the creator his monstrous passion, as the loved ones he neglected are murdered one after the other. After each death, he accuses himself and the monster in equal measure. When his friend Henry Clerval is found strangled, he is imprisoned and nearly executed as a result of his self-incriminating delirious outbursts. By the end, Frankenstein is as perfectly alone in the world as the monster, kept alive only by the guilty tie, fitted only for the mad pursuit across the arctic wastes during which the two figures merge into extinction.

In the novel, however, the doubling schema is complicated by the fact that the monster has a voice, unlike his better known cinematic counterpart. The heart of the book, most of the middle volume of the three-volume novel, is taken up with the creature's account of his pathetic and bewildered attempts to find his way in the world after his abandonment. He has by this stage committed his first crimes, murdering Frankenstein's young brother William and incriminating Justine, a beloved servant in the Frankenstein household, who is subsequently executed. Frankenstein suspects the true murderer, and when he encounters the monster during a walk in the mountains, loads him with abuse. The monster tells his story to extenuate his actions, and as an appeal to Frankenstein to recognize his responsibilities and improve the lot of his creation. He explains at length that his first impulses were good, that he longed for human sympathy, but that all his efforts to engage with others were met with horror and violence. The most sustained attempt was made when he found refuge in a hut adjoining a cottage, and, concealing himself there over many months, succeeded in learning how to speak, read and write from the inhabitants, an attractive and loving family, while secretly providing them with firewood and clearing the snow from their door. When he ventures to reveal himself, he is beaten and hounded away. The cottagers flee their home, and, symbolically, the enraged creature sets fire to it, vowing revenge on mankind in general, and his creator in particular. Now, with a mixture of threats and appeals for sympathy, he demands that Frankenstein creates for him a mate, with whom he will live 'cut off from the world'.

After some hesitation, Frankenstein agrees. He travels to a Scottish island at the very tip of Europe to fulfil his promise, but fear and loathing of the monster reassert themselves and he destroys the mate, initiating an all-out war which leads to the murders of Clerval, Frankenstein's bride Elizabeth and, indirectly, his already widowed father, from grief. There could be no reconciliation. Frankenstein refuses to acknowledge the rights of the being whom he verbally 'daemonizes'. The creature, though alive to the virtues of his victims, is hardened by despair.

They ultimately mirror each other in their single-minded dedication to hatred and revenge.

The recipient of both their stories is Robert Walton, a British polar explorer who glimpses the monster from a distance, driving a dog sleigh across the ice, and then picks up Frankenstein, who had become stranded and is found to be mortally ill. Walton's letters home to his sister Margaret begin and end the novel, and the narrations of Frankenstein and the monster are contained within them. By returning to the technique of encrypting tales of homicidal passion employed by Reeve and Radcliffe, Shelley would seem to draw back from the more daring practice of Baillie and Dacre, where criminal excess bursts the bounds of an overtly moralizing framework, and confronts the audience with little or no mediation. But the frame supplied by Walton is not an attempt to stabilize or recuperate the core narratives. Walton is himself a divided character, who seeks glory and new worlds, like Frankenstein, but also sustains familial bonds in his correspondence with his sister, and longs for a friend in his self-imposed exile. He is instantly, even passionately, drawn to Frankenstein, but the dying man prefers the role of mentor to that of brother. When, in the final section, Walton turns back from the quest which is the equivalent of Frankenstein's search for the secret of life, he does so unwillingly, to avoid a mutiny on his ship.

The final note is one of moral ambivalence. Frankenstein dies bequeathing the task of destroying the monster to Walton. Instantly the creature appears, and laments over the corpse, begging for pardon. Walton is sceptical; he calls to mind his friend's remarks about the creature's 'powers of eloquence and persuasion' and abuses him in terms Frankenstein would have used. Yet the monster is given the final word ('"Oh, it is not thus – not thus," interrupted the being') in a valedictory of great pathos, before disappearing into the night with the intention of immolating himself on a funeral pyre.

In this reading, I have not attempted to examine *Frankenstein* as a critique of 'masculinist' ideology, whether aesthetic, scientific or social – the most common approach in feminist discussion of the novel – though the revisions Shelley made to the 1831 edition certainly tend to bear out such readings. In the later version the description of Frankenstein's childhood and family life are more fully realized, and the figures of his mother and his adoptive sister and later bride, Elizabeth Lavenza, assume greater prominence, becoming the locus of feminine values overtly contrasted with the hero's ambitions. In the 1818 version, however, oppositional values – involving specifically an alternative model of creativity – are in fact centred on another man: Frankenstein's friend Henry Clerval.

Curiously, at the start of Frankenstein's confessional narrative, Elizabeth as a child is presented as the aesthetic counterpart to his scientific imagination, but is then immediately supplanted in this role by Henry. The distinction seems to be that she merely 'follows' the 'aërial creations of the poets' and peoples vacancy with her fantasies, while Henry, aged 9, actually '*wrote* a fairy tale, which was the delight and amazement of all his companions' (*F.* 21). In keeping with this initial double-take, his character remains strangely mutable. When Frankenstein goes to university, he is forced to remain at home by his businessman father, but he does not repine: 'he believed that a man might be a very good trader, and yet possess a cultivated understanding' (*F.* 28). Later, when Henry does eventually come to Ingolstadt, the apprentice man of commerce serves as loving nurse to the distraught Frankenstein. During their travels together through England and Scotland, Henry reverts to the type of the poet, 'His wild and enthusiastic imagination . . . chastened by the sensibility of his heart' (*F.* 130). After his untimely death, Frankenstein grieves the loss of the world of fancy that perished with the life of its creator. Henry appears to represent a utopian androgyny that transcends normal distinctions of gender. The sketchiness of his characterization suggests that Shelley was principally concerned with doing justice to her more flamboyant protagonists, but she would return to the task in her portrait of Euthanasia in *Valperga.*

The novel was published on 1 January 1818. On 11 March Mary and her family left for Italy, where she would spend the next five years. The publisher Lackington paid her only £28, but that was after the Shelleys' large bill for book purchases had been deducted. Interest in the novel developed quickly among the literati. Although it was anonymous, the dedication to William Godwin supplied a broad clue. Percy sent Walter Scott an advance copy, an action that paid dividends when a eulogy

131

by Scott appeared as lead review in the March issue of *Blackwood's Edinburgh Magazine*. After a detailed narration of the plot, he declared that 'the work impresses us with a high idea of the author's original genius', and added that, 'although such and so numerous have been the expedients for exciting terror employed by the romantic writers of the age', the novel 'shook a little even our firm nerves'. By its originality it 'excites new reflections and untried sources of emotion'.[17] This endorsement from one of the literary giants of the day – who was also a veteran of the Gothic craze of the 1790s – was a genuine triumph. It was marred only by Scott's assumption that the novel was the work of Percy. In spite of Mary's later claim, that she was 'very averse to bringing myself forward in print', she had no hesitation in putting him straight on this point when she wrote to thank him for the review, though in an appropriately modest manner.

The majority of the other reviews were also favourable, all echoing Scott's observations on the author's uncommon powers of mind and imagination. Even those few critics who condemned the work on the grounds that it provided no moral conclusion, conceded as much. The earliest negative criticism to appear was by John Wilson Croker in the Tory periodical the *Quarterly Review* in January. It was to be expected that any disciple of Godwin would receive short shrift from this quarter but, flatteringly, he complained that the outrage to taste and judgement was the greater in consequence of the writer's skill. Three months later Croker was to carry out his notorious critical assassination of Keats in the pages of the *Quarterly*. It is important here, as in the case of Joanna Baillie, to note that innovative female writers came in for attack in a similar measure to their male peers and counterparts, and that objections to their writing were not generally based on their sex. In the case of *Frankenstein* a number of reviewers besides Scott assumed that the author was male. But responses to later editions and other works, once Mary's authorship was known, were not on the whole marked by a sexual double standard.

For her next major work, during the period of pastoral calm at Marlow near Oxford in the autumn of 1817, Mary had conceived of a historical novel in the manner of Jane Porter and Walter Scott. But the idea was put by, in the disruption of the journey to

Italy, followed by a year of almost continual movement during which first the infant Clara, then 3-year-old William, tragically died. Through 1818 and 1819 Mary's literary impulses began to take a different direction, crystallizing in the novella *Matilda*, a tale of incestuous desire and suicidal remorse, which was written in the aftermath of William's death.

The traumatic circumstances in which the work was produced, and the refusal of Mary's father to undertake its publication (it would not be published until 1959) has meant that most interpretations have been insistently biographical. In some respects, admittedly, the narrative seems uncomfortably close to the bone. The heroine's mother dies soon after giving birth to her, as Mary's mother had done. And the heroine's feelings of guilt at the suicide of her father chime with Mary's own superstitious belief that the death of her children was somehow a punishment for the suicide of Harriet, Percy's first wife. But these elements also contribute to the internal thematic and formal coherence of the story. *Matilda* will be read here as a calculated progression from and extension of Shelley's intrepid literary début. Where could a writer of imagination go, when she had already stunned readers and critics with a work of brilliant originality? The topic of incest provided an answer: it was the *ne plus ultra* of Gothic writing.

Horace Walpole had followed up his success with *The Castle of Otranto* by writing a tragic drama centring on incest between a mother and her son. *The Mysterious Mother* was printed privately but effectively suppressed for many years by its own author, who invariably referred to its subject in his correspondence as 'revolting' and 'disgusting'. Nevertheless, Walpole probably revelled in the play's underground reputation; certainly he prided himself on having created, in the incestuous Countess of Narbonne, a character 'quite new on the stage'.[18] In *The Monk*, Lewis had extracted the last ounce of horror from the rape and murder of Antonia with the belated information that she was the sister of her attacker. In Shelley's own circle, a fascination with incest was part and parcel of a rebellious authorial persona. Rumours of an affair between Byron and his half-sister Augusta were no doubt reinforced by his publicly stated enthusiasm for *The Mysterious Mother* and hint at the theme in his own verse drama *Manfred* (1817). Shelley's epic poem *The Revolt of Islam*

(1818) originally concerned the incestuous love of Laon and Cythna, 'intended to startle the reader from the trance of everyday life', as the Preface averred. But references to incest were suppressed and the poem reissued after pressure from the publisher. Byron and the Shelleys were all pursued by the scandal arising from their summer by Lake Geneva, when it was reported that Mary and her 'sister' Claire shared their favours freely with their male companions in a 'League of Incest'.[19] Godwin's 'suppression' of *Matilda* must be understood in the context of literary precedent and personal scandal. He praised highly certain aspects of the story – notably the heroine's desperate pursuit of her father – but he also termed the work as a whole 'disgusting', as Walpole had done about *The Mysterious Mother*. This was a reasoned assessment that the work was too provocative and would damage Mary's promising career, and it was probably a correct one.

It is a tribute to Mary's desire to push further the exploration of emotional and moral extremes, that she did not herself foresee the dangers of publishing *Matilda*. She first began to apply herself to study of the literature of incest while visiting her parents' old friend Maria Gisborne in Leghorn in May 1818. It was from Mrs Gisborne that she received a copy of the 'Cenci manuscript', telling a true story from the Renaissance of the cruel and debauched Count Francisco Cenci, who had raped his daughter Beatrice and then been murdered by her. Mary translated it into a notebook. In the months that followed, Mary and Percy read Sophocles' *Oedipus* together and, at his suggestion, she began a translation of Alfieri's *Myrrha* (1785), a tragedy of incest between father and daughter, based on the story of Myrrha and Cinyras in Ovid's *Metamorphosis*. Each urged the other to write a play on Beatrice Cenci, and Percy eventually set to work, using Mary's translation and in consultation with her. *The Cenci* (1819) was to be her favourite among his writings. The most Gothic of his mature works, it was also the most commercially and critically successful. In this instance, the basis in historical fact seems to have alleviated the 'disgusting' nature of the plot, although it was not performed in his lifetime.

Matilda was first envisaged as one of a series of tales presented within an allegorical dream-vision in the manner of Dante's *Divine Comedy*. The draft of 'The Fields of Fancy' up to the end of

Matilda's story was written with great rapidity in August and September 1819. Shelley was by this time heavily pregnant. In November she received news of the latest of Godwin's endless financial disasters and, with the intention of giving him the profits from publication, began redrafting *Matilda* as an independent work three days before the birth of Percy Florence. She continued while nursing and finished the novella in February 1820. This crucial shift in the conception of the work had the result of emphasizing its Gothic elements and increasing its emotional impact. In the abandoned prologue of the first draft, the spirit of Matilda speaks of the tale of 'dark & phre[n]zied passions I must unfold' and of the struggle to find 'words burning enough to paint the tortures of the human heart', but the effect of the allegory is to sublimate the narrative of passion as a step on the ladder to wisdom.[20] The pedigree of the names, Matilda (*The Castle of Otranto*, Lee's *The Recess*, Radcliffe's *The Castles of Athlin and Dunbayne*, etc.), Elinor (*The Recess* again), and Lovel (Reeve's *The Old English Baron*, but changed to Woodville in Shelley's second version), suggest a Gothic novel fighting to get out. It was Shelley's need to make money that liberated the sensationalizing Gothic impulse from its philosophical shell.

As in *Frankenstein*, the design of *Matilda* involves the radical isolation of the main protagonist, in order to produce violent extremes of passion. No 'natural' (as opposed to supernatural) device could do this so effectively as incest, regarded as the ultimate crime against nature. The better to focus on the workings of subjectivity and bring out the full horror of the crime, Shelley kept the plot simple, almost without event (a technique also practised and theorized by Joanna Baillie in her *Plays on the Passions*). Matilda is dying, 'alone – quite alone – in the world'. At the start of the narrative she describes her 'strange state of mind': she is weak and feverish, but joyous at the thought of extinction. She wishes to relate her 'tragic history', although formerly she believed 'there was a sacred horror in my tale that rendered it unfit for utterance' (*M.* 5). The comparison she draws between herself and Oedipus about to die in the wood of the Eumenides gives an early hint at the content, and at the same time self-consciously alludes to a literary tradition, a history of the cathartic staging of passion.

The story is addressed to a dear friend, Woodville, whose identity will be made clear towards the end.

The first chapter is devoted to a portrait of her father. An independent fortune, unusual freedom in his youth, and a taste for novel-reading, all encouraged him to indulge his passions. An early affection for Diana, the daughter of a neighbouring gentleman, directed his passions towards good. She was steeped in the classics, had high ethical and political ideals, and served as his 'monitress'. They married, but only fifteen months later, after giving birth to Matilda, Diana was dead. He was plunged in despair and soon vanished, changing his name and travelling towards the East. This 'towering spirit' becomes almost a figure of legend for his friends.

Matilda is left in the care of an aunt, and spends the next sixteen years at her remote estate, on the shores of Loch Lomond in Scotland. She develops an ardent sensibility expressed in a passion for nature, and freely wanders in the countryside, climbing a nearby mountain and enjoying all the changes of the elements. Her formation is closely modelled on that of the hero of James Beattie's *The Minstrel*, which as we have noted, was a favourite work of Radcliffe (see p. 57). Sure enough, Matilda goes on to devour the writings of the chief geniuses of the canon of sublimity, Shakespeare and Milton, though this reading is interestingly balanced by Pope and works of ancient and classical history. In Gothic heroine mode, she becomes an adept at playing the harp. She takes refuge from her loneliness in day-dreams, imagining herself in the roles of Shakespearian and Miltonic romance, and forming 'aerial creations' of her own which often revolve around her mother and father. In her favourite fantasy, she dresses as a boy and goes to seek her father. Like Ellena in *The Italian*, she would wear his miniature on her breast, and when he recognized her – 'in a desert; in a populous city; at a ball; we should perhaps meet in a vessel' – his first words would be 'My daughter, I love thee' (*M*. 14).

On her sixteenth birthday, Matilda receives news that her father has returned, and he travels to Scotland to see her. She describes her own appearance, rowing across the Loch to meet him, 'dressed in white, covered only by my tartan *rachan* [wrap], my hair streaming on my shoulders, and shooting across with greater speed than it could be supposed I could give to my boat,

136

my father has often told me that I looked more like a spirit than a human maid' (*M*. 15). This visionary moment sets the tone for their future relations, the two of them bound in a mutual fantasy, but with Matilda herself assuming a superhuman and ultimately terrifying agency. Her father (he is given no other name) fulfils all her dreams, by his words, his appearance, and his passionate and concentrated affection. The few other characters who appear soon fall away, as if blasted by the intensity of their 'Paradisaical bliss' (*M*. 17). The aunt dies, and when they move to London, a suitor is quickly discouraged. But this latter event is the start of the Fall from Paradise. Overnight the father changes; he now avoids Matilda's company as strenuously as he once sought it. He retreats to the estate in Yorkshire where he had lived with his wife, but soon calls for Matilda to join him, and she goes there determined to discover the cause of his change of heart, and end the misery of doubt.

The denouement which next takes place – his revelation of incestuous desire, her recoil, his disappearance and her pursuit of him in a vain attempt to prevent suicide – is a crucial instance of female authorial power. All too often this episode has been misinterpreted as a display of the heroine's victimage, or even more naively, as a vicarious expression of Shelley's own sense of victimage. This is reductionism at its worst; the tactic of critics who prefer the role of amateur psychoanalyst to that of literary historian. The scenes of confession and pursuit are dense with allusion to literary precedent, and form a reflection on the whole tradition of women's Gothic.

Matilda relates most clearly to Baillie's dramatic practice, and particularly, to *De Monfort*, which was discussed in some detail in the previous chapter. The keystone of drama on this model is the construction of a character's private interiority, as a secret that must be penetrated. Immediately before the Fall, Matilda gains a fascinating insight into her father's inner torment, as he describes his reaction to the death of his wife.

> Even at that time I shuddered at the picture he drew of his passions: he had the imagination of a poet, and when he described the whirlwind that then tore his feelings he gave his words the impress of life so vividly that I believed while I trembled. I wondered how he could ever again have entered into the offices of life after his wild thoughts seemed to have given him affinity with the unearthly;

while he spoke so tremendous were the ideas which he conveyed that it appeared as if the human heart were far too bounded for their conception. His feelings seemed better fitted for a spirit whose habitation is the earthquake and the volcano than for one confined to a mortal body and human lineaments. (*M*. 18)

This account draws directly not only on the characterization of De Monfort, but also on Radcliffe's complex villains, Montoni and Schedoni. Schedoni's physiognomy in *The Italian* is sketched precisely as that of a sleeping volcano: 'it bore the traces of many passions, which seemed to have fixed the features they no longer animated' (*I*. 35). Matilda imagines that her father has changed, that he is 'now all love, all soft-ness... possessed by the gentlest passions' (*M*. 18). But she is soon disabused of this belief. She attempts to bridge the growing distance between them, but he repels her with the 'terrible emotions... he exhibited' (*M*. 19). It becomes her mission to force him to reveal the cause, just as Jane De Monfort forces into the open the secret of her brother, and brings about the catastrophe of the narrative.

Returning to the passage just quoted, it is necessary to recognize an extra dimension, which goes beyond Baillie and Radcliffe. This is not simply a description of the passions; it also reflects on the production and effect of such a description. The father is himself a Gothic writer. He has 'the imagination of a poet'; he is able to draw a 'picture' which makes Matilda tremble, which expands her mind to encompass the previously unimaginable, and causes her to suspend disbelief at the apparently unearthly. It is this experience of the sublime which she seeks to repeat by infiltrating the 'diseased yet incomprehensible state of his mind' (*M*. 20). In spite of her fear, she wants to possess and incorporate this strangeness.

Taking up the role of a Lady Macbeth, Matilda invokes the powers of darkness, positively summoning them into external being. She first catches a glimpse of the possibilities when she inadvertently praises Alfieri's *Myrrha*: 'I saw with affright that his whole frame shook with some concealed emotion that in spite of his efforts half conquered him' (*M*. 20–21; in *Myrrha*, it is the daughter who expresses incestuous desire for her father). Finally she insists outright on having the secret, disregarding his agonized pleas and dire warnings. Her strength of emotion overcomes his: 'I was led by passion and drew him with frantic heedlessness into the abyss that he so fearfully avoided' (*M.* 27). She falls at his feet and declares that she knows he hates her. He replies: ' "Yes, yes, I hate you! You are my bane, my poison, my disgust! Oh! No," And then his manner changed, and fixing his eyes on me with an expression that convulsed every nerve and member of my frame – "you are none of all these; you are my light, my only one, my life. – My daughter, I love you!" The last words died away in a hoarse whisper...'. The transference is complete. Her frame is convulsed as his had been. Her creative agency in the production of evil is underlined by the words he speaks: 'My daughter, I love you!'. Not only is this a speech-act forced by contradiction to her statement, but they are the very words generated by her imagination, when as a child she mentally wrote the script of their reunion. The only difference is in the change from 'thee' to 'you'; the difference between literary diction and impassioned performance.

Shelley's treatment of the relationship between father and daughter must not be confused with the problem of child abuse. What is at issue here is not a case of incest, but rather the representation of unnatural horror in a Gothic tale. Consequently, the question of responsibility and guilt needs to be approached quite differently. At the start of the story Matilda writes 'I record no crimes; my faults may easily be pardoned' (*M.* 6). But later, as she recalls her father's struggles against temptation, she accepts all the blame.

> My rashness gave the victory in this dreadful fight to the enemy who triumphed over him as he lay fallen and vanquished. I! I alone was the cause of his defeat and justly did I pay the fearful penalty. (*M.* 24)

Here, guilt is synonymous with creativity; it is what makes the story *her* story rather than his. It is a declaration of artistic ownership. She had claimed from her father 'a word! – I demand that dreadful word; though it be as a flash of lightning to destroy me, speak it' (*M.* 27). It did not destroy her but it destroyed him. After the event, she is the sole possessor of the 'sacred horror', the narrator of their joint history. The significance of lightning in Shelley's iconography first emerges in the scene at the beginning of *Frankenstein*, in which the spectacle of the destruction of an oak tree confirms the ambitious boy's desire to harness the forces of nature. Lightning can kill, but it also represents creative power, life-giving originality of mind. Matilda not only survives a bolt of lightning but, like Jove, comes to wield it.

Following the declaration, Matilda and her father part. She retires, terrified, to her room and resolves never to see him again. He prepares for a journey and leaves a letter full of remorse, giving her his blessing, and saying he will not return. This she immediately interprets as an intention to commit suicide. While the heavens rage stormily, she sets out in pursuit across country, by carriage and on foot, in a protracted, suspenseful sequence full of ambiguity. Is it a rescue mission or a manhunt? Matilda is overwhelmed with concern, but the earlier reference to the Eumenides, the Furies who punish crimes against nature, suggests other connotations. As they approach the sea at the end of the journey, Matilda turns to the steward who accompanies her and says, 'Mark, Gaspar, if the next flash of lightning rend not that oak my father will be alive' (*M*. 38). Instantly the oak is reduced to ashes. The father is discovered drowned.

For Shelley, the idea of incest between father and daughter is bound up with parricide. This is a feature of the Beatrice Cenci story, of *Matilda*, and of a closely related short story, 'The Mourner', published by Mary Shelley in the literary annual *The Keepsake* in 1829; and it is what distinguishes her treatment of the topic from that of Ovid and Alfieri, where it is the daughter who feels desire and destroys herself. In 'The Mourner' the 'murder' of the father is inadvertent – her obstinacy in refusing to be parted from him on the deck of a burning ship results in his death – but is nonetheless represented as parricide, for which the daughter must suffer torments of self-recrimination and a lonely and lingering decline. In *Matilda*, as we have seen, the heroine takes on the burden of guilt for drawing her father 'into the abyss', and similarly she turns herself into an anchorite, devoted to penitence. But, once again, the gesture is ambivalent: just as the extraction of confession was a display of power, so the murder of the father becomes an emblem of originality, a literal erasure of sources.

In the lengthy coda of the novella, Matilda manages to

extract herself from the duties and proprieties associated with her status as an heiress, by feigning death and going to live in a cottage in the north of England: 'It should be a solitary house on a wide plain near no other habitation: where I could behold the whole horizon, and wander far without molestation from the sight of my fellow creatures' (*M*. 44). Throughout, the emphasis is on her will and control, her conscious management of the situation. She lays aside some money for subsistence, arranges for a servant, surrounds herself with books and obtains a harp, adopts a 'fanciful nunlike dress' (*M*. 44); 'I was gathered up into myself' (*M*. 45). It is a repetition of her solitary childhood, but without joy, hope, or love, the sentiment that binds one to another. Matilda dedicates herself single-mindedly to the anticipation of death.

Her resolution is highlighted further by the apparently tangential introduction of Woodville, a poet bereaved by the death of his bride, who has similarly found a retreat in the wilderness. Matilda in relating the story seems to forget that it is addressed to Woodville, and tells his history in the third person. The portrait of him is reminiscent of Henry Clerval: a great genius, beloved by all, though unlike Clerval he follows his poetic vocation and achieves early success. Six months after the loss of the exquisite Elinor, he is already on the road to recovery, finding consolation in nature and exercise. It would seem that he is destined to redeem Matilda's loss as well, but Shelley steers resolutely away from this possibility. The heroine is deaf to his optimism and clings to her monstrosity:

> infamy and guilt was mingled with my portion; unlawful and detestable passion had poured its poison into my ears and changed all my blood, so that it was no longer the kindly stream that supports life but a cold fountain of bitterness corrupted in its very source. It must be an excess of madness that could make me imagine that I could ever be aught but one alone; struck off from humanity; bearing no affinity to man or woman; a wretch on whom Nature had set her ban. (*M*. 52–3)

In spite of mutual affection, their relationship is a curious battle of wills in which each seeks to incorporate the other in their own narrative web. Although she withholds her 'dark tale' from him, Matilda is tormented by the thought that he is using her for his own artistic ends, 'perhaps he is already planning a poem in which I am to figure . . . he takes all the profit and I bear all the burden' (*M.* 56). In retaliation she stages the scene for a suicide pact, procuring laudanum, placing it in two glasses and filling her room with flowers – 'decorat[ing] the last scene of my tragedy with the nicest care' (*M.* 57) – but unfortunately he declines to cooperate. When he is called away by his family, she seizes the initiative and reassumes authorial control by orchestrating a slow but certain death by self-neglect, passing the time by shaping her history into literary myth. Her final meditations involve a veritable fireworks display of quotes from Dante, Shakespeare, Coleridge and Wordsworth. As so often, 'original genius' must paradoxically manifest itself by providing appropriate terms of comparison.

THE AFTERMATH

Shelley's literary production from *Valperga* (1823) onwards shows an increasing turn away from Gothic. *Valperga* itself was written on a grander scale than her previous works, with a dual tendency towards voluminous historical detail on the Scott model, and broad philosophical allegory of a quite idiosyncratic kind. But it also contains markedly Gothic elements. Tilottama Rajan, in her excellent Introduction to the novel, has emphasized its debt – as a feminocentric blend of romance and history – to Sophia Lee's *The Recess*, and has also shown the links with Godwin's theory of fiction, closely akin to that of Joanna Baillie. The novel, as an analysis of the ruling passion of political ambition through the career of Castruccio Castracani, follows a path previously explored by Baillie in her two-part drama *Ethwald*. Here, ambition is pitted against the enthusiasm for political liberty of the heroine, Euthanasia, first the beloved of Castruccio, then his enemy. But the most vivid and unconventional character is that of Beatrice the prophetess, who becomes a convert to the Paterin belief in the prevailing power of evil. Godwin (who arranged the book's publication and made a few alterations to it) saw Beatrice, and a few minor figures suggestive of the marvellous and grotesque, as the chief triumphs of the work.[21]

With *The Last Man* (1826) Shelley went even further in the

direction of epic, presenting the spectacle of the complete destruction of the human species through plague and natural disaster in the last years of the twenty-first century. Horror is here universalized to a numbing degree, in a manner comparable to the vast apocalyptic canvases of the contemporary painter John Martin. Even in the more intimate preceding history of the circle surrounding Adrian, heir to the English throne, the complexity of relationships among a large cast of characters militates against the concentration of feeling found in the earlier works. Yet as an instance of sublime vision, the novel could be seen as the culmination of her Gothic ambitions. Certainly, the strangely haunting 'Author's Introduction' frames the narrative in this way, explaining it as the sum of the fragmentary outpourings of an ancient Sybil (a divine prophetess), which have been pieced together by the 'author' as a diversion from personal sorrow:

> My labours have cheered long hours of solitude, and taken me out of a world, which has averted its once benignant face from me, to one glowing with imagination and power...I confess, that I have not been unmoved by the development of the tale; and that I have been depressed, nay, agonized, at some parts of the recital, which I have faithfully transcribed from my materials. Yet such is human nature, that the excitement of mind was dear to me, and that the imagination, painter of tempest and earthquake, or, worse, the stormy and ruin-fraught passions of man, softened my real sorrows and endless regrets, by clothing these fictitious ones in that ideality, which takes the mortal sting from pain.[22]

The elegiac note is sustained throughout the novel by the narrator Lionel Verney, the Last Man himself. Inevitably, there have been many biographical readings equating Lionel and Mary Shelley, who in a few short years had seen the untimely deaths of two of her children, of her husband and his companion Edward Williams by drowning, and of Byron in Greece. More recently, critical attention has turned to the context of apocalyptic thinking at the time, for instance the debate on sustainable population carried out by Malthus and Godwin. Here I wish to return to Shelley's sense of loss and abandonment as it relates to her situation as a writer.

The Last Man, although it received some good reviews, was not a success commercially or, on the whole, critically. The work might be read on two levels, both as an allegory on literary isolation, and as a demonstration of it. The language used in the Introduction and quoted above – of 'imagination and power' and 'tempest and earthquake' and 'the stormy and ruin-fraught passions of man' – belongs to a Gothic sensibility which was fast becoming obsolete.[23] Shelley had made her first contribution to the genre when it was still at its height. She was then so young that when the vogue started to decline she was still only in her 20s; but all the peers and rivals, those who had shared in the culture of Gothic, had disappeared. By 1826 Percy Shelley, Byron, 'Monk' Lewis, Charles Maturin, Ann Radcliffe, Charlotte Dacre were all dead. In a few more years Walter Scott and Sarah Siddons would be gone. Joanna Baillie remained, but now published little and was herself regarded as the relic of a past generation. Godwin continued to publish, and father and daughter supported each other in their endeavours, as they attempted to maintain a foothold in a changing literary marketplace.

One obvious route was barred for many years: her hostile father-in-law Sir Timothy Shelley refused to let her edit and publish her husband's writings almost until his death in 1844, at the age of 91. As a consequence, she was thrown back on her own resources to supplement the stingy annuity Sir Timothy permitted her and her son Percy Florence, and compelled to adapt and survive as a writer in this inhospitable climate. She published three more novels, *Perkin Warbeck* (1830), *Lodore* (1835), and *Falkner* (1837); the first, another stab at historical romance, the others domestic fictions which gained sententious approval from some reviewers, pleased to see her imagination tamed. Apart from a late travel journal, *Rambles in Germany and Italy* (1844), the rest was essentially hack-work: reviews and encyclopaedia biographies and short stories for the literary annuals, which annoyed her by their constraints, and wore her down. Many of the stories are in fact very accomplished, but they were nevertheless work by rote. The custom was for writers to spin tales to fit elegant engravings produced in advance, and though this could be a stimulus, they were severely restricted by word limits. Through the late 1820s and early 1830s Shelley produced a string of such stories with Gothic themes: 'Ferdinando Eboli' (1829), concerning a scheming double; 'Transformation' (1830), about a hot-headed young man who switches bodies with an evil dwarf; 'The Dream' (1831), which features a superstitious young countess; and 'The Mortal Immortal' (1833), in which the apprentice of the alchemist Cornelius Aggripus discovers he has accidentally drunk the elixir of immortality and must outlive his beloved. However, increasingly the potential for affect is undercut by the humorously knowing tone of the narration.

In 1831, at the advanced age of 34, Mary Shelley wrote the Introduction to the 'Bentley's Standard Novels' edition of *Frankenstein*, attempting to explain the former self who had been capable of creating it: 'My husband ... was for ever inciting me to obtain literary reputation, which even on my own part I cared for then, though since I have become infinitely indifferent to it' (*F.* 193). It is endearing to find that she could be unfashionably extreme even in her indifference. But the previous year she published a review of her father's latest novel *Cloudesley*, which suggests that at some level she 'kept faith' with the ideals and ambitions of her youth. She describes how Godwin 'transfuses himself into the very souls of his pers+onages; he dives into their secret hearts, and lays bare, even to their anatomy, their workings; not a pulsation escapes him', how, comparing this book to others 'we felt as if we had quitted gardens and parks, and tamer landscapes, for a scene on nature's grandest scale; that we wandered among giants' rocks'. The writer 'rapts us from ourselves, filling our bosoms with new and extraordinary emotions, while we sit soul-enchained by the wonders of his art'.[24] Whether or not this is a sincere assessment of the novel, there is no mistaking Shelley's enduring enthusiasm for a style of writing and of reading which by the 1830s must indeed have had the air of an outlandish geological remnant of a distant epoch. This was the age of Bulwer Lytton and Catherine Gore, and the witty, sophisticated Silver-Fork Novel, which dealt in the brittle dialogue and surfaces of high society. It was the age of Felicia Hemans and Letitia Landon ('L.E.L.'), whom one might call professional women as well as professional writers, since their success depended upon foregrounding their sex at every opportunity, and on their demarcation of the specific and limited sphere of female agency. Yet in spite of this realization Shelley retained a sense of the permanent relevance of those experiments which had characterized women's Gothic, continuing to sign each new title page 'by the Author of "Frankenstein"'. In her final novel she has her tormented anti-hero say, 'Is passion known in these days? Such as I felt, has any other experienced it? The expression has fled from our lips; but it is as deep-seated as ever in our hearts.'[25]

Notes

INTRODUCTION

1. This was Horace Walpole's coinage in the Preface to the second edition of *The Castle of Otranto*, in 1765.
2. 'On the Supernatural in Poetry', *New Monthly Magazine*, 16 (1826), 145–52; reprinted in Folger Collective on Early Women Critics (ed.), *Women Critics 1660–1820* (Bloomington and Indianapolis: Indiana University Press, 1995), 331–8; p. 331.
3. Pat Rogers, '"Towering Beyond Her Sex": Stature and Sublimity in the Achievement of Sarah Siddons', in Mary Ann Schofield and Cecilia Macheski (eds.), *Curtain Calls: British and American Women and the Theater 1660–1820* (Athens, OH: Ohio University Press, 1991), 48–67; p. 50.
4. Folger Collective, *Women Critics*, 333–4.
5. Thomas Campbell, *Life of Mrs Siddons* (London: Edward Moxon, 1839), 121.
6. Siddons did in fact play Hamlet on a number of occasions. One of Garrick's talent scouts, the Rev. Henry Bate, wrote to him in 1775, 'beware yourself, *Great Little Man*, for she plays Hamlet to the satisfaction of Worcestershire critics'; later she acted the role to great acclaim in Birmingham, Manchester, Bath and Dublin, but never in London. See A. Kennard, *Mrs Siddons* (London: W. H. Allen, 1887), 29, 49–51.
7. Folger Collective, *Women Critics*, 334.
8. Folger Collective, *Women Critics*, 334.
9. See Alan Richardson, 'Romanticism and the Colonization of the Feminine', in Anne Mellor (ed.), *Romanticism and Feminism* (Bloomington and Indianapolis: Indiana University Press, 1988), 13–25; and Diane Long Hoeveler, *Romantic Androgyny: The Women Within* (University Park, PA, and London: Penn State University Press, 1990).
10. Judith Pascoe, *Romantic Theatricality: Gender, Poetry, and Spectatorship* (Ithaca and London: Cornell University Press, 1997), 21.

11. In addition to Pascoe and Rogers, for interesting contextualizations see Paula R. Backscheider, *Spectacular Politics* (Baltimore and London: Johns Hopkins University Press, 1993), 204–15, and Julie A. Carlson, *In the Theatre of Romanticism* (Cambridge: Cambridge University Press, 1994), 162–75.

12. On the subtleties of the argument, see John Barrell's account in 'Imaginary Treason and Imaginary Law: Treason Trials in 1794', *The Birth of Pandora and the Division of Knowledge* (London: Macmillan, and Philadelphia: University of Pennsylvania Press, 1992), 119–43.

13. Her biographer Boaden, conscious of the resonance, said of the royal command performance in 1785 that 'The audiences of this period were sufficiently decorous to be trusted with a scenic display of regal assassination' (James Boaden, *Memoirs of Mrs Siddons*; (London: Gibbings and Company, 1896), p. 317.

14. Campbell, *Life*, 195.

15. Campbell, *Life*, 185, and Kennard, *Mrs Siddons*, 117.

16. Siddons's 'Remarks' are included in Campbell, *Life*, 170.

17. Boaden, *Memoirs*, 308.

18. James Sheridan Knowles's account, cit. Dennis Bartholomeusz, *Macbeth and the Players* (Cambridge: Cambridge University Press, 1969), 120–21.

19. Boaden, *Memoirs*, 318.

20. Campbell, *Life*, 171.

21. John Bell's report, cit. Bartholomeusz, *Macbeth*, 107.

22. The poem is included in Jerome J. McGann (ed.), *The New Oxford Book of Romantic Period Verse* (Oxford and New York: Oxford University Press, 1993), 37–9.

23. Two recent investigations of the status of the passions in the period are Alan T. McKenzie, *Certain, Lively Episodes: The Articulation of Passion in Eighteenth-Century Prose* (Athens and London: University of Georgia Press, 1990), and Adela Pinch, *Strange Fits of Passion: Epistemologies of Emotion, Hume to Austen* (Stanford: Stanford University Press, 1996).

24. Murray, Peter and Linda Murray, *The Penguin Dictionary of Art and Artists* (4th edn., Harmondsworth, 1976), 251.

25. Nicholas Penny (ed.), *Reynolds* (London: Weidenfeld & Nicolson, 1986), 325.

26. Cit. Margaret S. Carhart, *The Life and Works of Joanna Baillie*, Yale Studies in English, 64 (New Haven: Yale University Press, 1923), 191.

27. John Waldie, UCLA MSS, vol. 4, 169/8 (4 July 1789), 4; cit. Jeffrey N. Cox (ed.), *Seven Gothic Dramas 1789–1825* (Athens, OH: Ohio University Press, 1992), 53.

28. Reviewed in *Critical Review*, 61 (1786), 317. I thank Antonia Forster for drawing my attention to the work.

29. Cit. in 'Sarah Siddons', in Philip J. Highfill Jr., Kalman A. Burnim and Edward A. Langhans (eds.), *A Biographical Dictionary of Actors, Actresses et al.* (Carbondale: South Illinois Press, 1991), vol. XIV, 22.

30. Leslie A. Marchard (ed.), *Byron's Letters and Journals*, 12 vols. (Cambridge: Harvard University Press, 1975–1982), vol. V, p. 203.

31. Cit. Gretchen Rous Besser, *Germaine de Staël Revisited* (New York: Twayne Publishers, 1994), 11.

32. P. P. Howe (ed.), *The Complete Works of William Hazlitt*, vol. V, *A View of the English Stage* (London and Toronto: J. M. Dent and Sons, 1930), 312.

33. Boaden, *Memoirs*, 305–6.

34. Cit. Campbell, *Life*, 295.

35. Highfill et al., 'Sarah Siddons', vol. XIV, pp. 12–14.

36. Ellen Donkin cites Wally Outen and James Boaden in 'Mrs Siddons Looks Back in Anger: Feminist Historiography for Eighteenth-Century Theater', *Critical Theory and Performance*, ed. Janelle G. Reinelt and Joseph R. Roach (Ann Arbor: University of Michigan Press, 1992), 281, 282.

37. Penny, *Reynolds*, 385.

38. Cit. Highfill et al., *Biographical Dictionary*, vol. XIV, p. 18.

39. *Monthly Review*, 32 (May 1765), 394.

40. Raymond Williams, *Modern Tragedy* (London: Chatto & Windus, 1966), 27.

CHAPTER 1. CLARA REEVE AND SOPHIA LEE

1. *Monthly Review*, 58 (January 1778), 85.

2. *Critical Review*, 45 (April 1778), 316.

3. Horace Walpole, *The Yale Edition of Horace Walpole's Correspondence*, ed. W. S. Lewis, 48 vols. (New Haven: Yale University Press, 1973–83), vol. 28, pp. 381–2.

4. Anna Laetitia Barbauld, *The British Novelists*, vol. XXII (London, 1810), p. ii.

5. *British Critic*, 2 (1793), 383.

6. *Gentleman's Magazine* (1768), vol. I, pp. 15–16.

7. Edmund Burke, *A Philosophical Enquiry into the Origin of our Ideas of the Sublime and Beautiful*, ed. James Boulton (Oxford: Basil Blackwell, 1987), 38.

8. It appears as the frontispiece to the third volume of *Edward, ou le Spectre du Château* (Paris, [1800?]). The same scene is illustrated in the English seventh edition of the novel in 1802, but in this case the contents of the trunk are discreetly concealed from view.

9. 'Obituary of Ann Radcliffe', *Annual Register* (1824).

10. Cit. Kennard, *Mrs Siddons*, 52.
11. Highfill et al., *Biographical Dictionary*, vol. XIV, p. 7.
12. Frances Burney, *Diary and Letters of Madame D'Arblay*, 7 vols. (London: Henry Colburn, 1842), vol. I, p. 400.
13, Ian Gilmour, *Riots, Risings and Revolution: Governance and Violence in Eighteenth-Century England* (London: Pimlico, 1993), 342–3.
14. Boaden, *Memoirs*, 126.
15. *Dictionary of National Biography*.
16. Although Prévost d'Exiles provided an important precedent, for instance with the novel *Cleveland* (1731–9) concerning a fictional illegitimate son of Cromwell, this was not remarked by reviewers.
17. See Paul Ranger, '*Terror and Pity reign in every Breast*': *Gothic Drama in the London Patent Theatres, 1750–1820* (London: Society for Theatre Research, 1991), 90–105.
18. Sophia Lee, *Almeyda, Queen of Granada* (London: Cadell and Davies, 1796), 6.
19. For differing evaluations of the merit of the scene, see Ranger, *Gothic Drama*, 55–6, and Backscheider, *Spectacular Politics*, 170.
20. See John K. Reeves, 'The Mother of *Fatherless Fanny*', *English Literary History*, 9 (September 1942), 224–33.

CHAPTER 2. ANN RADCLIFFE

1. [Cassandra Cooke], *Battleridge: An Historical Tale, Founded on Facts*, 2 vols. (London: Cawthorn, 1799), vol. I, p. viii; Nathan Drake, *Literary Hours: or Sketches, Critical, Narrative, and Poetical*, 2 vols. (2nd edn. 1800; repr. New York, 1970), vol. I, p. 359.
2. Review of *The Italian*, *Analytical Review*, 25 (1797), 516.
3. Michel Foucault, 'What Is an Author?', trans. J. V. Harari, *The Foucault Reader*, ed. Paul Rabinow (Harmondsworth: Penguin, 1986), 114.
4. Frederick Page (ed.), *Letters of John Keats* (London: Oxford University Press, 1954), 90.
5. Washington Irving, *Journals and Notebooks*, ed. Nathalia Wright (Madison: University of Wisconsin Press, 1969), vol. I, pp. 55–6.
6. Deborah D. Rogers, *Ann Radcliffe: A Bio-Bibliography* (Westport and London: Greenwood Press, 1996), and Richter Norton, *Mistress of Udolpho: The Life of Ann Radcliffe* (New York and London: Leicester University Press, 1999).
7. Jane Austen, *Northanger Abbey*, ed. John Davie (Oxford: Oxford University Press, 1980), 82.
8. 'Estimate of the Literary Character of Mrs Ann Ratcliffe [sic]', *Monthly Magazine*, 47 (1819), 125–6; p. 126.
9. William Duff, *Essay on Original Genius* (London: Edward and Charles

Dilley, 1767), 141.

10. William Duff, *Letters on the Intellectual and Moral Character of Women* (Aberdeen: for the author, 1807), 29–30.

11. *British Critic*, 30 (1807), 544.

12. In the novel, the 'Song of a Spirit' is not attributed to Adeline, but to servants of the marquis, who is attempting to seduce her (*R.* 161–2).

13. See E. J. Clery, 'Ann Radcliffe and D. A. F. de Sade: Thoughts on Heroinism', in *Women's Writing*, 1:2 (1994), 203–14.

14. Montagu Pennington (ed.), *Letters from Mrs Elizabeth Carter to Mrs Montagu between the Years 1755 and 1800*, 3 vols. (London: Rivington, 1817), vol. III, pp. 322–5. I am indebted to Deborah Rogers, *Anne Radcliffe: A Bio-Bibliography*, for useful references on the reception of Radcliffe among the bluestockings.

15. *Letters of Anna Seward*, 6 vols. (Edinburgh: Constable and Co.; London: Longman, Hurst, Rees et al., 1811), vol. III, pp. 388–90.

16. Katherine C. Balderston (ed.), *Thralina: The Diary of Mrs Hester Lynch Thrale (Later Mrs Piozzi)* (Oxford: Clarendon Press, 1942), vol. II, pp. 885–7.

17. Cit. James Clifford, *Hester Lynch Piozzi (Mrs Thrale)* (1941; New York: Columbia University Press, 1987), 379.

18. Ioan Williams (ed.), *Sir Walter Scott on Novelists and Fiction* (New York: Barnes and Noble, 1968), 103.

19. Williams, *Walter Scott on Novelists*, 105.

20. Williams, *Walter Scott on Novelists*, 104.

21. Edwin W. Marrs, Jr. (ed.), *The Letters of Charles and Mary Anne Lamb* (Ithaca and London: Cornell University Press, 1976), vol. II, p. 279. For more on the excitement generated by Radcliffe's earnings see Norton, *Mistress of Udolpho*, 94–7.

22. *Monthly Magazine*, 47 (1819), 125–6.

CHAPTER 3. JOANNA BAILLIE AND CHARLOTTE DACRE

1. Cit. Margaret S. Carhart, *The Life and Works of Joanna Baillie*, Yale Studies in English, 64 (New Haven: Yale University Press, 1923), 15. See also Norton, *Mistress of Udolpho*, 185–7.

2. Cit. Carhart, *Joanna Baillie*, 17.

3. Cit. Carhart, *Joanna Baillie*, 15.

4. *Quarterly Review*, cit. Carhart, *Joanna Baillie*, 17.

5. Ellen Donkin's chapter on Baillie in *Getting Into the Act* (London: Routledge, 1995) is the prime example; she lays great emphasis on Piozzi's statements that by revealing her identity and therefore her sex Baillie opened herself to spiteful criticism, but fails to provide any persuasive evidence. The current dominant reading of Baillie by

critics such as Anne Mellor and Catherine Burroughs suggests that she was self-marginalized, that is, writing from a position of conscious subordination and gendered critique; with this inter- pretation, too, I would disagree. Gender politics is not the beginning and end of Baillie's audacious challenge to theatrical orthodoxy. She was simply the most visionary and influential dramatist of her day.

6. See Carhart, *Joanna Baillie*, 47–52, which counters Donkin's very partial version.

7. 'Lines to Agnes Baillie on Her Birthday', *The Dramatic and Poetical Works of Joanna Baillie* (London: Longman, Brown, Green and Longmans, 1851), 811.

8. Some of the poems were later included in revised form in *Fugitive Verses* (1740). See Roger Lonsdale's remarks in *Eighteenth-Century Women Poets: An Oxford Anthology* (Oxford and New York: Oxford University Press, 1989), 429–30.

9. Notably Bertrand Evans, *Gothic Drama from Walpole to Shelley* (Berkeley and Los Angeles: University of California Press, 1947); Paul Ranger, *Terror and Pity*; and Jeffrey N. Cox (ed.), *Seven Gothic Dramas, 1789–1825* (Athens: Ohio University Press, 1992), which contains the text of *De Monfort*.

10. Joseph W. Donohue, *Dramatic Character in the English Romantic Age* (Princeton: Princeton University Press, 1970), 81.

11. A formulation repeated by Baillie in *De Monfort*, IV. ii. 26–7.

12. Cit. Carhart, *Joanna Baillie*, 64–5; Harriet Martineau, *Autobiography*, ed. M. W. Chapman (Beston, 1877), vol. I, p. 270.

13. Evans, *Gothic Drama*, 201.

14. Evans, *Gothic Drama*, 201.

15. Cit. Carhart, *Joanna Baillie*, 116.

16. See Campbell, *Mrs Siddons*: 'Joanna Baillie has left a perfect picture of Mrs Siddons, in her description of *Jane de Monfort*' (p. 303).

17. See Carhart, *Joanna Baillie*, 121–2.

18. See Carhart, *Joanna Baillie* (pp. 128–42), on the stage history of De Monfort after the original Drury Lane production. Cox, *Seven Gothic Dramas* (pp. 55–7), has an interesting discussion of Siddons as a dramatic interpreter of Gothic, but sees her acting style as typically passive, in contrast to Paula Backscheider, and myself. Baillie returned the compliment in an ode addressed 'To Mrs Siddons', 'our tragic queen', praising especially the subtlety and variety of her depictions of the passions.

19. At the time, Byron was a member of the management committee at Drury Lane.

20. Another strategy of containment in the first performed version was the Epilogue, written by the Duchess of Devonshire. In the most conventional terms, it urges the audience to 'bid the scene's dread

horror cease/And hail the blessing of domestic peace'. It is included in Cox, *Seven Gothic Dramas*, 313–14.

21. From *Poems* (1790), reproduced in Lonsdale, *Eighteenth-Century Women Poets*.
22. Carhart, *Joanna Baillie*, 29.
23. The poem is included in Jerome M. McGann (ed.), *The New Oxford Book of Romantic Period Verse*, (Oxford and New York: Oxford University Press, 1993).
24. Her obituary in *The Times*, 9 November 1825, reports that 'Mrs Byrne [Charlotte Dacre], wife of Nicholas Byrne of the *Morning Post*', died on 'Monday evening in Lancaster Place, after a long and painful illness, which her purity and sublime greatness of soul enabled her patiently and piously to endure'.
25. Charlotte Dacre, *Confessions of the Nun of St Omer: A Tale*, intr. Devendra P. Varma, 2 vols. (1805; repr. New York, 1972), vol. I, p. 3.
26. Dacre's identification as Charlotte King was questioned until Adriana Craciun drew attention to the fact that poems published in *Hours of Solitude* also appear in *Trifles of Helicon*; see '"I hasten to be disembodied": Charlotte Dacre, the Demon Lover, and Representations of the Body', *European Romantic Review*, 6:1 (Summer 1995), 75–97, p. 90.
27. See Donald Reiman, Introduction to *Hours of Solitude* (1805; repr. New York: Garland, 1978), pp. vii–viii.
28. The recurrence of certain favourite 'romance' names in *Trifles of Helicon*, and Charlotte and Sophia's shared lexicon of words like 'enhorrored' and 'enanguished', suggest the possible existence of a childhood fantasy-world comparable to that of the Brontës. Ann Jones, without knowing they were sisters, noted the similarity of Sophia's style; see 'Charlotte Dacre', in *Ideas and Innovations: Best Sellers of Jane Austen's Age* (New York: AMS, 1986), 224–49; 320 n. 54.
29. Cox, *Seven Gothic Dramas*, 225.
30. Craciun, '"I hasten to be disembodied"'.
31. Other poems on the same theme, but with a male speaker, are 'The Lover's Vision' (*HS* i. 51) and 'How Canst Thou Doubt', signed 'Azor' (*HS* ii. 27).
32. See Lucyle Werkmeister, *A Newspaper History of England 1792–93* (Lincoln: University of Nebraska Press, 1967), 33. Werkmeister also outlines King's involvement in the world of newspaper-publishing (p. 32).
33. Ann Jones has established the outlines of Dacre's connection with Byrne in *Ideas and Innovations*, 224–49.
34. Lewis was forced by the public outcry to tone down later editions of *The Monk*; it was passages of irreligion he excised, rather than of overt sexuality.

35. Dacre's later novel *The Passions* (1811) returns to the theme of literary corruption; the villainous Appollonia Zulmer vengefully leads Julia astray by exposing her to Rousseau's *Nouvelle Héloïse*.
36. 'Dacre' is apparently a pseudonym, but the name used by critics today.
37. *Monthly Literary Recreations*, 1 (July 1806), 80.
38. See above, p. 93.
39. Robert Miles, *Gothic Writing 1750–1820: A Genealogy* (London and New York: Routledge, 1993), 181.
40. Craciun has usefully discussed it in the context of the contemporary medical discourse on nymphomania (Introduction, *Zofloya* by Charlotte Dacre (Peterborouogh, Ontario: Broadview, 1997), 21–2).
41. Miles, *Gothic Writing*, 187; Diana Long Hoeveler, *Gothic Feminism: The Professionalization of Gender from Charlotte Smith to the Brontës* (University Park, PA: Pennsylvania State University Press, 1998), 155.
42. Backscheider, *Spectacular Politics*, 212–14. Ranger, *'Terror and Pity'*, (pp. 94–8), shows other images of Siddons in the role and gives a detailed account of her acting style in the play.
43. Kennard, *Mrs Siddons*, 77–8.
44. Captain Friedrich von Hassell, quoted in John Alexander Kelly, *German Visitors to English Theatres in the Eighteenth Century* (Princeton, 1936), 145.
45. In *The Monk*, both Matilda and Beatrice de las Cisternas wield a knife, but they are liminal figures, supernatural or legendary. In the play *Adelgitha*, Lewis added a foonote to explain that a tyrant-slaying female character was not the heroine of the piece; supposedly extenuating information.
46. *The General Review of British and Foreign Literature*, vol. 1 (London: D. N. Shury, 1806), included in Craciun, (ed.), *Zofloya*, 263.
47. *Morning Post*, 25 April 1807; cit. Jones, *Ideas and Innovations*, 225.

CHAPTER 4.   MARY SHELLEY

1. Walpole, *Castle of Otranto*, 9–10.
2. Claire Clairmont, quoted in Mrs Julian Marshall, *The Life and Letters of Mary Wollstonecraft Shelley*, 2 vols. (London: Bentley & Son, 1889), vol. II, p. 248.
3. Mary Wollstonecraft, *'Mary' and 'The Wrongs of Woman'*, ed. Gary Kelly (Oxford and New York: Oxford University Press, 1976), 144.
4. William Godwin, *Caleb Williams* (Oxford and New York: Oxford University Press, 1982), 1.
5. Ibid.
6. Folger Collective, *Women Critics*, 302.

7. See Richard Holmes, *Shelley: The Pursuit* (1974; Harmondsworth: Penguin, 1987), 14; Holmes draws on Thomas Medwin, *The Life of Percy Bysshe Shelley* (1847).

8. Walter Peck has shown systematically the numerous parallels in Appendix A of *Shelley: His Life and Work*, 2 vols. (Boston and New York: Houghton Mifflin, 1927), vol. II, pp. 305–13.

9. Roger Ingpen and Walter E. Peck (eds.), *The Complete Works of Shelley*, 10 vols. (New York: Gordian Press, 1965), vol. VIII, p. 18.

10. Emily W. Sunstein, *Mary Shelley: Romance and Reality* (Baltimore: Johns Hopkins University Press, 1989), 84.

11. Paula R. Feldman and Diana Scott-Kilvert (eds.), *The Journals of Mary Shelley 1814–1844*, 2 vols. (Oxford: Oxford University Press, 1987), vol. I, p. 48.

12. *Journals*, vol. I, pp. 32–3.

13. *Journals*, vol. I, pp. 54–5.

14. Thomas Moore, *Letters and Journals of Lord Byron*, 2 vols. (London: John Murray, 1830), vol. II, p. 31; cit. Sunstein, *Mary Shelley*, 121.

15. Sunstein, *Mary Shelley*, 126.

16. See for instance Burton R. Pollin, 'Philosophical and Literary Sources of *Frankenstein*', *Comparative Literature*, 17:2 (Spring 1965), 97–108; Anne K. Mellor, 'A Feminist Critique of Science', in *Mary Shelley: Her Life, Her Fiction, Her Monsters* (London and New York: Routledge, 1988), 89–114; D. S. Neff, 'The "Paradise of the Mothersons": *Frankenstein* and *The Empire of the Nairs*', *Journal of English and Germanic Philology*, 955 (1996), 204–22.

17. Scott, Williams (ed.), *Walter Scott on Novelists*, 271, 272.

18. Walpole, *Correspondence*, vol. 28, p. 9.

19. See Sunstein, *Mary Shelley*, 119 etc. see index.

20. Mary Shelley, 'The Fields of Fancy', in vol. II of Pamela Clemit (ed.), *The Novels and Selected Works of Mary Shelley* (London: Pickering & Chatto, 1996), 359.

21. See Tilottama Rajan, Introduction, *Valperga* by Mary Shelley (Peterborough, Ontario: Broadview Press, 1998), 21.

22. Mary Shelley, *The Last Man*, ed. Morton D. Paley (1826; Oxford, 1994), 8–9.

23. Robert D. Mayo used the frequency of 'Gothic' stories in the *Lady's Magazine* as an index of the genre's span of popularity, but his terminal date of 1813–14 seems premature given the success of later works by Charles Maturin, James Hogg, and Shelley herself. ('How Long Was Gothic Fiction in Vogue?', *Modern Language Notes*, 58, January 1943, pp. 58–64).

24. *Blackwood's Edinburgh Magazine*, XXVII (May, 1830), 712, 713; reprinted in *Works of Mary Shelley*, vol. II, 203, 204.

25. *Works of Mary Shelley*, vol. VII, 156.

Select Bibliography

Under the heading 'Selected Texts by the Author', I have listed primary texts relevant to the study of Gothic writing in the most easily available modern editions; or failing this, I have referred to an early edition.

CLARA REEVE

Selected Texts by the Author

Original Poems On Several Occasions (London, 1769).
The Old English Baron: A Gothic Story, ed. James Trainer (1778; London, 1967). A revised version of *The Champion of Virtue* (1777).
The Progress of Romance (1785; facsimile repr., New York, 1970).
The Exiles, or Memoirs of the Count de Cronstadt (London, 1788).
Memoirs of Sir Roger de Clarendon (London, 1793).

Critical and Biographical Studies

Barbauld, Anna Laetitia, 'Clara Reeve', in *An Essay on The Origin and Progress of Novel Writing; and Prefaces, Biographical and Critical from 'the British Novelists'* (London, 1820).

Berg, Temma F., 'Engendering the Gothic: Clara Reeve Redecorates *The Castle of Otranto*', *Reader* 44 (Spring 2001), 53–78.

Casler, Jeanine, 'The Primacy of the "Rougher" Version: Neo-Conservative Editorial Practices and Clara Reeve's *The Old English Baron*', *Papers on Language and Literature* 37:4 (Fall 2001), 404–37.

Clery, E. J., *The Rise of Supernatural Fiction* (Cambridge, 1995), 83–9.

Ehlers, Leigh, 'A Striking Lesson to Posterity: Providence and Character in Clara Reeve's *The Old English Baron*', *Enlightenment Essays*, 9 (1978), 62–76.

Gentleman's Magazine, Obituary, II (1807), 1233.

Lee, Elizabeth, 'Clara Reeve', *Dictionary of National Biography*, 63 vols. (London, 1885–).

Scott, Walter, 'Clara Reeve' (1823), in Ioan Williams (ed.), *Sir Walter Scott on Novelists and Fiction* (London, 1968).

Watt, James, *Contesting the Gothic: Fiction, Genre, and Cultural Conflict, 1764–1832* (Cambridge, 1999), 42–69.

SOPHIA LEE

Selected Texts by the Author

The Recess (1783–5; facsimile repr., New York, 1972).
Warbeck (Dublin, 1786).
The Hermit's Tale (London, 1787).
Almeyda, Queen of Granada (London, 1796).
The Recess, ed. April Alliston (Lexington, KY, 2000).

Critical and Biographical Studies

Donkin, Ellen, *Getting into the Act: Women Playwrights in London, 1776–1829* (London, 1995).

Doody, Margaret Ann, 'Deserts, Ruins, Troubled Waters: Female Dreams in Fiction and the Development of the Gothic Novel', *Genre*, 10 (1977), 529–72.

Isaac, Megan Lynn, 'Sophia Lee and the Gothic of Female Community', *Studies in the Novel*, 28:2 (1996), 200–18.

Lewis, Jayne Elizabeth, '"Ev'ry Lost Relation": Historical Fictions and Sentimental Incidents in Sophia Lee's *The Recess*', *Eighteenth-Century Fiction*, 7:2 (1995), 165–84.

Mann, David D, and Susan Garland Mann, with Camille Garnier, 'Sophia Lee', in *Women Playwrights in England, Ireland and Scotland 1660–1823* (Bloomington and Indianapolis, 1996).

Nordius, Janina, 'A Tale of Other Places: Sophia Lee's *The Recess* and Colonial Gothic', *Studies in the Novel* 34:2 (Summer 2002), 162–76.

Spencer, Jane, *The Rise of the Woman Novelist* (Oxford, 1986), 195–201.

ANN RADCLIFFE

Selected Texts by the Author

The Castles of Athlin and Dunbayne, ed. Alison Milbank (1789; Oxford and New York, 1995).

A Sicilian Romance, ed. Alison Milbank (1790; Oxford and New York, 1993).

The Romance of the Forest, ed. Chloe Chard (1791; Oxford and New York, 1986).

The Mysteries of Udolpho, A Romance, ed. Bonamy Dobrée, intr. and notes Terry Castle (1794; Oxford and New York, 1998).

The Italian, or the Confessional of the Black Penitents, A Romance, ed. Frederick Garber, intr. and notes E. J. Clery (1797; Oxford and New York: Oxford University Press, 1988).

Gaston de Blondeville (London, 1826).

Critical and Biographical Studies

Castle, Terry, 'The Spectralization of the Other in *The Mysteries of Udolpho*', in Laura Brown and Felicity Nussbaum (eds.), *The New Eighteenth Century* (London, 1987), 237–53), and Terry Castle, *The Female Thermometer: Eighteenth Century Culture and the Invention of the Uncanny* (Oxford and New York, 1995), 120–39.

Chaplin, Sue, 'Romance and Sedition in the 1790s: Radcliffe's *The Italian* and the Terrorist Text', *Romanticism* 7:2 (2001), 177–90.

Cottom, Daniel, *The Civilized Imagination: A Study of Ann Radcliffe, Jane Austen, and Sir Walter Scott* (Cambridge, 1985).

Durant, David, 'Ann Radcliffe and the Conservative Gothic', *Studies in English Literature*, 22 (1982), 519–29.

Gautier, Gary, 'Ann Radcliffe's *The Italian* in Context: Gothic Villains, Romantic Heroes, and a New Age of Power Relations', *Genre* 32:3 (Fall 1999), 201–24.

Gonda, Caroline, *Reading Daughter's Fictions 1709–1834: Novels and Society from Manley to Edgeworth* (Cambridge, 1996), 140–73.

Grant, Aline, *Ann Radcliffe: A Biography* (Denver, 1951).

Howells, Coral Ann, 'The Pleasures of the Woman's Text: Ann Radcliffe's Subtle Transgressions in *The Mysteries of Udolpho* and *The Italian*', in Kenneth W. Graham (ed.), *Gothic Fictions: Prohibition/Transgression* (New York, 1989), 158–61.

Kelly, Gary, 'A Constant Vicissitude of Interesting Passions: Ann Radcliffe's Perplexed Narratives', *Ariel*, 10 (1979), 45–64.

McIntyre, C. F., *Ann Radcliffe in Relation to Her Time* (New Haven, 1920). Worth consulting.

Miles, Robert, *Ann Radcliffe: The Great Enchantress* (Manchester and New York, 1995). A stimulating account of the novels, historically and theoretically informed.

Murray, E. B., *Ann Radcliffe* (New York, 1972).

Norton, Rictor, *Mistress of Udolpho: The Life of Ann Radcliffe* (London and New York, 1999). The definitive biography, based on exhaustive research.

Rogers, Deborah D., *Ann Radcliffe: A Bio-Bibliography* (Westport, CT, and London, 1996). A useful guide to the contemporary reception of Radcliffe's work, as well as modern criticism, though already outdated by the pace of new publications.

Rogers, Deborah, D. (ed.), *The Critical Response to Ann Radcliffe* (London and Westport, CT, 1994). A valuable anthology.

Stoler, John F., *Ann Radcliffe: The Novel of Terror and Suspense* (New York, 1980).

Tompkins, J. M. S., *The Work of Mrs Radcliffe and its Influence on Later Writers* (1921; repr. New York, 1980). Worth consulting.

Ware, Malcolm, *Sublimity in the Novels of Ann Radcliffe* (Uppsala and Copenhagen, 1963).

JOANNA BAILLIE

Selected Texts by the Author

A Series of Plays, in which it is attempted to Delineate the Stronger Passions of the Mind (London, vol. I, 1798, vol. II, 1802, vol. III, 1812). Known as *Plays on the Passions*.

'Introductory Discourse' from *Plays on the Passions* (1798), in Folger Collective on Early Women Critics (ed.), *Women Critics 1660–1820: An Anthology* (Bloomington and Indianapolis, 1995).

Cox, Jeffrey N. (ed.) *De Monfort: A Tragedy* (1798), in *Seven Gothic Dramas 1789–1825* (Athens, OH, 1992).

Orra (1812); repr. Cambridge: Chadwyck-Healey English Verse Drama Full-Text Database, 1994.

The Dramatic and Poetical Works of Joanna Baillie: Complete in One Volume (London, 1851).

Breen, Jennifer (ed.) *The Selected Poems of Joanna Baillie 1762–1851* (Manchester and New York, 1999).

Critical and Biographical Studies

Anderson, Julie, 'Spectacular Spectators: Regendering the Male Gaze in Delariviere Manley's *The Royal Mischief* and Joanna Baillie's *Orra*', *Enculturation: A Journal for Rhetoric, Writing, and Culture* 3:2 (Fall, 2001), n.p.

Brewer, William D., 'Joanna Baillie and Lord Byron', *Keats-Shelley Journal*, 44 (1995), 165–81.

—— 'The Prefaces of Joanna Baillie and William Wordsworth', *Friend: Comment on Romanticism*, 1:2–3 (1991–2), 34–47.

Bugajski, Ken A., *Joanna Baillie: An Annotated Bibliography*, in *Romanticism On the Net*, 12 (November, 1988). No pagination. Online. Internet. <http://users.ox.ac.uk/~scat0385/bwpbaillie.html>. The essential starting point for any detailed study of Baillie.

Burroughs, Catherine B., *Closet Stages: Joanna Baillie and the Theater Theory of British Romantic Women Writers* (Philadelphia, 1997). An impressive account of Baillie's work.

—— (ed.), *Women in British Romantic Theatre: Drama, Performance, and Society, 1790–1840* (Cambridge, 2000). Contains essential essays on Baillie, including Jeffrey N. Cox's 'Baillie, Siddons, Larpent: Gender, Power, and Politics in the Theatre of Romanticism'.

Carhart, Margaret S., *The Life and Works of Joanna Baillie*, Yale Studies in English, 64 (New Haven, 1923). Still the best biographical study.

Cox, Jeffrey N., Introduction, *Seven Gothic Dramas 1789–1825* (Athens, OH, 1992).

Donkin, Ellen, *Getting into the Act: Women Playwrights in London, 1776–1829* (London, 1995). A lively and provocative account.

Donohue, Joseph, W., Jr., *Dramatic Character in the English Romantic Age* (Princeton, 1970).

——— *Theatre in the Age of Kean* (Oxford and Totowa, NJ, 1975).

Evans, Bertrand, *Gothic Drama from Walpole to Shelley*, University of California Publications, 18 (Berkeley, 1947).

Gamer, Michael, *Romanticism and the Gothic: Genre, Reception, and Canon Formation* (Cambridge, 2000), 127–62.

Henderson, Andrea, 'Passion and Fashion in Joanna Baillie's "Introductory Discourse"', *PMLA*, 112 (1997), 198–213.

Howells, Coral Ann, *Joanna Baillie and Her Circle, 1790–1850: An Introduction* (London, 1973).

Inchbald, Elizabeth, 'Remarks [An Introduction to *De Monfort*]', in E. Inchbald (ed.), *The British Theatre, or, A Collection of Plays*, vol. 24 (London, 1808), 3–6.

Mellor, Anne, K., 'A Criticism of Their Own: Romantic Women Literary Critics', in John Beer (ed.), *Questioning Romanticism* (Baltimore and London, 1995), 29–48.

——— 'Joanna Baillie and the Counter-Public Sphere', *Studies in Romanticism*, 33 (1994), 559–67.

Page, Judith W., *Wordsworth and the Cultivation of Women* (Berkeley, 1994).

Purinton, Marjean D., *Romantic Ideology Unmasked: The Mentally Constructed Tyrannies in Dramas of William Wordsworth, Lord Byron, Percy Shelley, and Joanna Baillie* (Newark, 1994).

——— 'Socialized and Medicalized Hysteria in Joanna Baillie's *Witchcraft*', *Prism 9* (2001), 139–56.

Ranger, Paul, *'Terror and Pity Reign in Every Breast': Gothic Drama in the London Patent Theatres, 1750–1820* (London, 1991). Valuable contextualization.

Ross, Marlon B., *The Contours of Masculine Desire: Romanticism and the Rise of Women's Poetry* (New York, 1989).

Watkins, Daniel P., *A Materialist Critique of English Romantic Drama* (Gainesville, FL, 1983).

Yudin, Mary F., 'Joanna Baillie's Introductory Discourse as a Precursor of Wordsworth's Preface to Lyrical Ballads', *Compar(a)ison*, (1994), 101–11.

CHARLOTTE DACRE

Selected Texts by the Author

And Sophia King, *Trifles of Helicon* (London, 1798).

Confessions of the Nun of St Omer: A Tale, intr. Devendra P. Varma, 2 vols. (1805; repr. New York, 1972).

Hours of Solitude: A Collection of Original Poems, now first published, intr. Donald Reiman (1805; repr. New York, 1978).

Zofloya; or, The Moor, ed. Adriana Craciun (1806; Peterborough, Ont., 1997).

Zofloya; or, The Moor, ed. Kim Ian Michasiw (1806; Oxford and New York, 1997).

The Libertine (1807; repr. New York, 1974).
The Passions (1811; repr. New York, 1974).

Critical and Biographical Studies

Byron, George Gordon, 'English Bards and Scotch Reviewers' (1809), in E. H. Coleridge (ed.), *The Works of Byron*, 7 vols. (London: John Murray, 1898).
Craciun, Adriana, '"I hasten to be disembodied": Charlotte Dacre, the Demon Lover, and Representations of the Body', *European Romantic Review*, 6:1 (Summer 1995), 75–97. Pioneering criticism of Dacre's poetry.
Dunn, James, A., 'Charlotte Dacre and the Feminization of Violence', *Nineteenth-Century Fiction* 53:3 (Dec. 1998), 307–27.
Hoeveler, Diane Long, *Gothic Feminism: The Professionalization of Gender from Charlotte Smith to the Brontës* (Pennsylvania, 1998), 143–58.
Jones, Ann, 'Charlotte Dacre', in *Ideas and Innovations: Best Sellers of Jane Austen's Age* (New York, 1986), 224–49. The best biographical account, to which Craciun has added.
McGann, Jerome J., '"My Brain is Feminine": Byron and the Poetry of Deception', in Andrew Rutherford (ed.), *Byron: Augustan and Romantic* (Basingstoke, 1990), 26–51.
Mellor, Anne K., 'Interracial Sexual Desire in Charlotte Dacre's *Zofloya*', *European Romantic Review* 13:2 (June 2002), 169–73.
Miles, Robert, *Gothic Writing 1750–1820: A Genealogy* (London and New York, 1993), 179–88.
Peck, Walter Edwin, Appendix 8: 'Shelley's Indebtedness in *Zastrozzi* to Previous Romances', in *Shelley: His Life and Work*, 2 vols. (Boston and New York, 1927), vol. II, 305–9.
Summers, Montague, 'Byron's Lovely Rosa', in *Essays in Petto* (Edinburgh, 1928).
—— Introduction to Charlotte Dacre, *Zofloya, or The Moor* (London, 1928).
Wilson, Lisa M., 'Female Pseudonymity in the Romantic "Age of Personality": The Career of Charlotte King/Rosa Matilda/Charlotte Dacre', *European Romantic Review* 8:2 (Spring 1997), 393–420.

MARY SHELLEY

Selected Texts by the Author

Frankenstein or The Modern Prometheus (The 1818 Text), ed. Marilyn Butler (Oxford and New York, 1994).
Matilda (written 1819–20), ed. Pamela Clemit, vol. 2 of *The Novels and Selected Works of Mary Shelley*, general ed. Nora Crook (London, 1996).
Valperga; or, The Life and Adventures of Castruccio, Prince of Lucca, ed. Tilottama Rajan (1823; Peterborough, Ont., 1998).
The Last Man, ed. Morton D. Paley (1826; Oxford, 1994).

Mary Shelley: Collected Tales and Stories, ed. Charles E. Robinson (Baltimore and London, 1976).

Critical and Biographical Studies

Allen, Graham, 'Beyond Biographism: Mary Shelley's *Matilda*, Intertexuality, and the Wandering Subject', *Romanticism* 3:2 (1997), 170–84.

Baldick, Chris, *In Frankenstein's Shadow: Myth, Monstrosity and Nineteenth-century Writing* (Oxford, 1987). A fascinating account of the novel's impact, as myth, on social and political analysis.

Botting, Fred, *Making Monstrous: Frankenstein, Criticism, Theory* (Manchester, 1991). A post-structuralist reading which explores the ramifications of 'monstrosity'.

—— *Frankenstein: Contemporary Critical Essays* (Macmillan, 1995). Useful collection of rival interpretations, including an extensive bibliography.

Conger, Syndy M., (ed.) *Iconoclastic Departures: Mary Shelley After 'Frankenstein'* (Madison, NJ, 1997).

Davis, William, 'Mathilda and the Ruin of Masculinity', *European Romantic Review* 13:2 (June 2002), 175–81.

Edelman-Young, Diana, ' "Kingdom of the Shadows": Intimations of Desire in Mary Shelley's *Mathilda*', *Keats-Shelley Journal* 51 (2002), 116–44.

Frank, Frederick, S. (ed.), 'Mary Shelley's *Frankenstein*: A Register of Research', *Bulletin in Bibliography*, 4 (1983), 163–87.

Levine, George, and U. C. Knoepflmacher, *The Endurance of Frankenstein: Essays of Mary Shelley's Novel* (Berkeley, 1979). Contains some key pioneering treatments of the novel and its socio-historical context.

Lyles, W. H., *Mary Shelley: An Annotated Bibliography* (New York and London, 1975).

Johnson, Barbara, 'My Monster/My Self', *Diacritics*, 12 (1982), 2–10.

Mellor, Anne K., *Mary Shelley: Her Life, Her Fiction, Her Monsters* (London and New York, 1988). By an influential feminist critic.

—— (ed.), *The Other Mary Shelley: Beyond 'Frankenstein'* (Oxford, 1993).

Moers, Ellen, *Literary Women* (1963; new edn. London, 1978). Pioneering feminist bio-criticism.

Paulson, Ronald, 'Gothic Fiction and the French Revolution', *English Literary History*, 48 (1981), 532–54. Oft-cited historicist treatment.

Poovey, Mary, ' "My Hideous Progeny": Mary Shelley and the Feminisation of Romanticism', *PMLA*, 95 (1980), 332–47.

Spark, Muriel, *Child of Light: A Reassessment of Mary Wollstonecraft Shelley* (Hadleigh, Essex, 1951); reprinted in revised form as *Mary Shelley: Romance and Reality* (London, 1988).

Sunstein, Emily W., *Mary Shelley: Romance and Reality* (Boston, 1989). The most comprehensive biography; it seeks, successfully, to establish Shelley as a significant literary figure in her own right.

GENERAL READING

Bibliographies

Fisher, Benjamin, F., *The Gothic's Gothic: Study Aids to the Tradition of the Tale of Terror* (London, 1988).

Frank, Frederick S., *The First Gothics: A Critical Guide to the English Gothic Novel* (New York and London, 1987).

—— *Gothic Fiction: A Master List of Twentieth-Century Criticism and Selected Texts* (London, 1988).

——, *Guide to the Gothic: an Annotated Bibliography of Criticism* (Metuchen, NJ, 1984).

——, *Guide to the Gothic II, an Annotated Bibliography of Criticism 1983–1993* (Lanham, MD, 1995).

Gamer, Michael, *Romanticism and the Gothic: Genre, Reception, and Canon Formation* (Cambridge, 2000).

Hoeveler, Diane Long and Tamar Heller (eds.), *Approaches to Teaching Gothic Fiction: the British and American Traditions* (New York, 2002).

Hogle, Jerrold E. (ed.), *The Cambridge Companion to Gothic Fiction* (Cambridge, 2002).

McNutt, D. J., *The Eighteenth-Century Gothic Novel: An Annotated Bibliography of Criticism and Selected Texts* (Folkestone, 1975).

Punter, David (ed.), *A Companion to the Gothic* (Oxford, 2000).

Spector, Robert Donald, *The English Gothic: A Bibliographic Guide to Writers from Horace Walpole to Mary Shelley* (London and Westport, CT, 1984).

Summers, Montague, *A Gothic Bibliography* (New York, 1941).

On Gothic Writing

Baker, E. A., *The Novel of Sentiment and the Gothic Romance, The History of the English Novel*, vol. 5 (New York, 1929).

Birkhead, Edith, *The Tale of Terror: A Study of the Gothic Romance* (London, 1921).

Botting, Fred, *Gothic* (London and New York, 1996).

Bruhm, Steven, *Gothic Bodies: The Politics of Pain in Romantic Fiction* (Philadelphia, PA, 1994).

Castle, Terry, *The Female Thermometer: Eighteenth-Century Culture and the Invention of the Uncanny* (Oxford and New York, 1995).

Clery, E. J., *The Rise of Supernatural Fiction, 1762–1800* (Cambridge, 1995).

—— and Robert Miles (eds.), *Gothic Documents: A Sourcebook (1700–1820)* (Manchester, 2000).

Day, William Patrick, *In the Circles of Fear and Desire: A Study of Gothic Fantasy* (Chicago and London, 1985).

Delamotte, Eugenia, *Perils of the Night: A Feminist Study of Nineteenth-Century Gothic* (New York and Oxford, 1990).

Ellis, Kate F., *The Contested Castle: Gothic Novels and the Subversion of Domestic Ideology* (Urbana, IL, and Chicago, 1989).

Fleenor, Juliann E. (ed.), *The Female Gothic* (Montreal and London, 1983).

Graham, Kenneth W., (ed.), *Gothic Fictions: Prohibition/Transgression* (New York, 1989).

Haggerty, George E., *Gothic Fiction/Gothic Form* (University Park, PA, and London, 1989).

Hoeveler, Diane Long, *Gothic Feminism: The Professionalization of Gender from Charlotte Smith to the Brontës* (University Park, PA, 1998).

Howard, Jacqueline, *Reading Gothic Fiction: A Bakhtinian Approach* (Oxford, 1994).

Howells, Coral Ann, *Love, Mystery and Misery: Feeling in Gothic Fiction* (1978; 2nd edn. London, 1996).

Jacobs, Edward, *Accidental Migrations: An Archaeology of Gothic Discourse* (Bucknell, 2000).

Kelly, Gary, *English Fiction of the Romantic Period, 1789–1830* (London and New York, 1989).

Kiely, Robert, *The Romantic Novel in England* (Cambridge, MA, 1972).

Kilgour, Maggie, *The Rise of the Gothic Novel* (London and New York, 1995).

Lévy, Maurice, *Le Roman 'Gothique' Anglais, 1764–1824* (1968; new edn. Paris, 1996).

McNutt, Dan, *The Eighteenth-Century Gothic Novel: An Annotated Bibliography of Criticism and Selected Texts* (Folkestone, 1975).

Miles, Robert, *Gothic Writing 1750–1820: A Genealogy* (London and New York, 1993).

—— (ed.), *Female Gothic Writing*, special number of *Women's Writing*, 1:2 (1994).

Napier, Elizabeth, *The Failure of Gothic: Problems of Disjunction in an Eighteenth-Century Literary Form* (Oxford, 1987).

Punter, David, *The Literature of Terror*, 2 vols. (1980; 2nd edn. London and New York, 1996).

Railo, Eino, *The Haunted Castle: A Study of the Elements of English Romanticism* (London and New York, 1927).

Sage, Victor, *Horror Fiction in the Protestant Tradition* (Basingstoke and London, 1988).

Sedgwick, Eve K., *The Coherence of Gothic Conventions* (New York, 1980).

Summers, Montague, *The Gothic Quest: A History of the Gothic Novel* (London, 1938).

Todorov, Tzvetan, *The Fantastic: A Structural Approach to a Literary Genre* (Ithaca, NY, 1975).

Tompkins, J. M. S., *The Popular Novel in England, 1770–1800* (London, 1932).

Varma, Devendra, P., *The Gothic Flame* (London, 1957).

Williams, Anne, *Art of Darkness: A Poetics of Gothic* (Chicago and London, 1995).

Index